Highland Paths

Tales of Glengarry

By
Kenneth J. McKenna

Inside front and back cover: Highland Scene. Engraving: The Clachan of Aberfoil and Loch Ard, Scotland - William Miller, 1868.

Highland Paths

Tales of Glengarry

By
Kenneth J. McKenna

Canadian Cataloguing in Publication Data

McKenna, Kenneth J., 1931-
    Highland Paths: Tales of Glengarry

Stories and articles from the Highland Paths columns of the
    Glengarry News, Alexandria, Ont., 1992-1995, re-edited
    and expanded.
ISBN 0-9695824-3-9

    1. Scots--Ontario--Glengarry--History. 2. Immigrants--
Ontario--Glengarry--History. 3. Glengarry (Ont.)--Emigration
and immigration--History. 4. Highlands (Scotland)--
Emigration and immigration--History. 5. Scots--North
America--History. I. Title.

FC3095.G55Z7 1998   971.3'750049163   C98-901250-6
F1059.G5M34 1998

Design and Typography by Louise Sproule, Vankleek Hill, Ontario.

Printed and bound in Canada by
Tri-Graphic Printing (Ottawa) Ontario.

Acknowledgements

My wife Anne and I have been partners since we first met almost 50 years ago. We have always shared a common interest in the Scots and the Scots Highlanders, in particular, their Irish origins and the place of the Gael in Canadian history. We have visited those areas of interest to us in the British Isles and Ireland on many occasions, living for brief periods in the Hebrides and in the Western Highlands. Through good times and bad she has stubbornly stood by me and it is to her that I owe everything that is good in my life, including much of the preliminary computer work on this book. Our daughter Sine has helped immensely with her knowledge of Gaelic which she first acquired in our home in Montreal, at St. Francis Xavier University in Antigonish, NS and from her years of living on the Isle of Skye.

In the production of this book the advice, encouragement and support of David Anderson, past president of *The Glengarry Historical Society*, has been invaluable. He has helped me along every step of the way. Others who deserve recognition for their help are local historians Bernie MacCulloch of Glen Roy, Donald Simon Fraser of Lochinvar, Harold MacMillan of Hawkesbury, Dr. Hugh P. MacMillan of Guelph, Bob Campbell of Ottawa, Gaelic experts Deborah and David Livingston-Lowe of Toronto, Bill McIntyre, publisher, and Lindsay Cameron, advertising manager, *The Glengarry News* and Lucy Chisholm Theoret, Hélène Quesnel and Brenda Goulet who set up my columns every week in the paper. Hugh Allan MacMillan, Patch and Duncan A. Macdonell and Gertrude (Mrs. Gerald Paddy) McDonald contributed to the list of Glengarry nicknames.

Tales, memories and anecdotes about Glengarry have inspired the background of most of my Highland Paths stories. Among many who have shared this information with me are Ewen (Angus Katie) McDonald, Angus Rory MacDonald of St Raphael's, the late Neil MacLeod, Marguerite and Gerald McGillis, Hugh Allan McDonald, Charles McDonald, Eileen and Jim Seay and Gaelic speakers Alec MacDonald (6th of Kenyon) and the late Gilbert MacRae.

Two old friends who have influenced me greatly are Lauchlin MacInnes, whose Gaelic-English poem *The Gaelic Voice in Canada* is a classic and whose 1984 booklet *Glengarry and Western Gaelic* captures the essence of Glengarry; and historian Rory MacDonald of Spean Bridge, Scotland. I have known Rory for over 30 years and have learned much about Lochaber and the Keppoch (Glen Roy) MacDonalds from him.

James Hunter, the Highland historian and author of *A Dance Called America* (see Suggested Reading List at the end of this book) has visited us on several occasions and has been an important inspiration to me.

For financial help I am indebted to Kevin Macdonald, president of *The Glengarry News* and his brother, Allan and to Grant Campbell QC. Alan D. MacKinnon's support in every way is gratefully acknowledged.

A special thanks goes to publisher Louise Sproule for her patience and expertise in putting this book together.

— Kenneth J. McKenna

Introduction

Most of these stories and articles first appeared in the Highland Paths columns of the Glengarry News of Alexandria, Ontario, from 1992 to 1995, re-edited and expanded by me for this book. A few have not been previously published. They are all based on the Highland Scots background of the area, where Gaelic was the language of most of the people for many generations.

Glengarry, the easternmost county of Ontario on the St Lawrence River, originally extended to the Ottawa River. Settlers began arriving in the 1780s, exiles from the American Revolution, soon joined by others who came directly from Scotland. Some were disbanded soldiers and their families. They named their new home Glengarry in memory of the area from which many of them originated in the Western Highlands of Scotland. Within 50 years, there were about 20,000 Gaelic-speaking Highland Scots in Greater Glengarry, about the same number as in Cape Breton..

Topics covered in these articles include conditions in Scotland relevant to the Highland people and why they left their native land, how they adapted to a new way of life, and what has happened to their descendants in the past two hundred years. The stories are not only about well-known historical characters and noted personages, but about ordinary people as well.

I have tried to flesh out the dry bones of history with stories that explain the unique background of the Highland people; their Gaelic language and music, their traditions and heritage, their place in Canada. I am not a professional historian. My knowledge comes from others and from a 60-year acquaintanceship with the themes of my articles. On more than twenty trips to the Scottish Highlands and Cape Breton my wife Anne and I have amassed a great deal of information from many friends and local historians and have done much research on the culture of the Gael in particular and of the Celt in general.

My ability in the Gaelic language is limited. The only musical instruments that I have ever played are the piano and pipes, with a little experience with the violin. I also sing in the Glengarry Gaelic Choir. But I have been blessed with a wife who is a real pianist and composer and who has a much better ability than I in the language. Our daughter Sine, a Gaelic singer, has spent some years in the Highlands, and is quite fluent in Gaelic. They both teach the language and music of the Gael. Joanne, another daughter, is a prize-winning Gaelic singer and her sister Brigid has studied in Wales and has developed an interest in the culture of that other Celtic nation.

The identity of the Gaelic Scots has been so muddled over the years by romanticism, myth, inaccuracy and just plain lies that even the Scots themselves are often confused. It is hoped that these stories will dispel much of that confusion and be entertaining as well.

Most Gaelic family and place names are no longer written in Gaelic. When the proper Gaelic spelling is used in this book, it is rendered in *italics*, followed by phonetics, such as Glengarry - *Gleann garaidh*, Glown-uh Garr-eh. In Scottish Gaelic, the first syllable of a word is stressed, as in LAGG-an. When two words are combined, as in the name Glengarry, they are both given equal stress — GLEN GARR-y. Apart from subtle differences in pronunciation which are difficult to imitate in print, the most common problem for non-Gaelic speakers is the written *ch* sound. It is pronounced softly, as in *loch.*

In olden times the word "Highland" (capitalised when it refers to the specific area) meant mountainous country and "Highlanders" described the people who lived there, regardless of their language. There are no equivalent words in Gaelic. The Gaelic-speaking Scots were described thusly because, by the 15th century, they had gradually been forced into the more remote and hilly areas of the west and north of Scotland. Any who remained in the non-Gaelic areas were quickly swallowed up in the Lowland culture.

We know that Gaelic was once predominant in Scotland because most of the placenames there are of Gaelic origin. The only exceptions were the areas of Strathclyde, on both shores of the upper River Clyde, where the language was a Brytonic tongue related to Welsh; the Lothian area around Edinburgh, which had a strong Anglo-Saxon element, and the eastern part of Caithness and the islands of Orkney and Shetland, where the Norse influence was dominant.

Even in the south-west of Scotland in the now completely Lowland area of Galloway there were pockets of Gaelic-speakers as recently as the 18th century.

Scottish Gaelic is an offshoot of Irish Gaelic and came to Scotland around the 5th century with the Dalriadic Scots from Ireland. To make matters more complicated, these early Gaels (or Celts, a Greek term they would not have known), met an even older people in Scotland, the Picts. Very little is known of these earlier people; we don't even know for certain what they called themselves; perhaps it was something that sounded like "Pict" or perhaps the name derived from the Latin for "painted," because they evidently dyed their bodies blue with woad, a plant of the mustard family. Their language was a form of Celtic which could be understood, with some difficulty, by the Gaelic newcomers.

In the 16th century, before the word "Highland" was widely used, the Gaelic-speaking people of Scotland were often referred to as "wylde Irish" and their language called Irish or misnamed "Erse," a word now mercifully seen only in crossword puzzles.

To forestall any danger of unity between Scots and Irish Gaels, the word "Highland" was promoted to convince the Scottish Gaels that they were unconnected with their Irish cousins. It was a brilliant ploy. The wedge between the two peoples remains to this day.

As the Lowland language, derived from much the same Germanic sources as English, gradually became dominant in Scotland, Gaelic declined until it now survives only in the more remote areas of the Highlands and Islands and in parts of Cape Breton.

To a Gaelic-speaker, you are a Gael, *Gàidheal*, if it is your native tongue or if your ancestors spoke it, and a *Gall*, a stranger, otherwise. More specifically, a non-Gael, whether in Scotland or England, is known as *Sasunnach*, a Saxon, with or without a sneer. And the area known as the Highlands in English, is *Gàidhealtachd*, Gael-tahkt, the land of the Gael, in the Gaelic language.

The Gaelic Scots were not always perceived as the romantic heroes portrayed by Sir Walter Scott two centuries ago. Before he almost single-handedly rescued them from obloquy, they were often the objects of fear, misunderstanding, and even hatred.

His best-sellers and the exploits of Highland regiments in the British army changed it all. Even tartan and kilts, banned after the Jacobite Rising of 1745, eventually became the symbols of all Scotland.

But under the surface of this new-found goodwill lurked attitudes and actions that were to destroy the old Gaelic way of life forever. The Highland chiefs and the kinship which supported the clan system were gone after Culloden. The clanspeople were forced, in one way or another, to leave their native hills. Thus Glengarry began.

The changes to the old Gaelic way of life were described in the late 18th by the outstanding English scholar Samuel Johnson:

> There was perhaps never any change of national manners so quick, so great, and so general, as that which has operated in the Highlands, by the last conquest, [1746] and the subsequent laws. We came thither too late to see what we expected, a people of peculiar appearance, and a system of antiquated life . . . Of what they had before the late conquest of the country, there remains only their language and their poverty. Their language is attacked on

every side. Schools are erected, in which *English* only is taught, and there were lately some who thought it reasonable to refuse them a version of the holy scriptures, that they might have no monument of their mother-tongue . . .

— Dr. Samuel Johnson, *A Journey to the Western Islands of Scotland,* 1773.

In recent years the Canadian-born author and television personality Robert MacNeil wrote of the decline of Irish Gaelic in 19th century Ireland, a situation almost identical to what happened to Scottish Gaelic:

Gaelic-speaking children were punished with wooden gags, and subjected to mockery and humiliation. Brothers were encouraged to spy on sisters. Under the regime of the tally-sticks, the child would wear a stick on a string round its neck. Every time the child used an Irish Gaelic word, the parents would cut a notch in the wood. At the end of the week, the village schoolmaster would tally up the notches and administer punishment accordingly. There was only one end in view: the eradication of Irish. The schools became the instrument of oppression, just as, ironically, they are today the chief promoters of Gaelic . . .

— Robert MacNeil, *The Story of English.*

The articles in this book were intended to be self-contained, and do not have to be read in any particular order, but have been grouped under four categories for convenience. There is naturally some overlapping themes and phrases which run throughout, and I have left them intact. I hope that the reader does not find such repetitions tedious or annoying.

The Highland Scots were, to a large extent, a displaced people. To paraphrase the closing words of the great BBC film Culloden, directed by Peter Watkins and produced by the BBC:

But wherever they went, to the disease-ridden slums of the south, to the lumber camps of Canada, or to the stockyards of Australia, they brought their music, their poetry, their language, and their children with them.

Contents

Language, Music and Poetry

Glengarry Clans, Families and Local Heroes

Appendix

Scotland

The Door of Achallader

How history comes alive

The death of Alexandria pharmacist Frank McLeister this year (1992) reminded me of my friend Col. Archie Fletcher in Scotland and the strange tale of a castle door.

This is how the MacLeisters (Fletcher in English, *Mac-an-fhleisdeir* in the original Gaelic) lost their castle of Achallader in the Highlands of Scotland. The clan name means the son of the arrow maker, an important trade when bows and arrows were used as weapons.

The Fletchers of Achallader were a small clan, their lands situated near Glenorchy, to the east of Glencoe. They were neighbours of the powerful Campbells of Breadalbane.

Some four centuries ago, Black Duncan Campbell of the Cowl, seventh Laird of Glenorchy, coveted the Fletcher territory and decided to add their castle and lands to his own vast estate.

In a time when robber barons were the rule rather than the exception, Black Duncan was one of the worst. Even his fellow Campbells feared and hated him and he robbed them as readily as he robbed his traditional enemies.

He planned his treacherous strategy against the Fletchers carefully. Leading a party into the hills on a stag hunt, he deliberately delayed their return until, late in the day and far from home, they found themselves near Achallader Castle. Keeping himself out of sight, Black Duncan sent one of his servants, a recently employed Lowlander who had no Gaelic, to ride down, tether his horse in front of the castle, and ask for accommodation.

The innocent man did as he was told. Suddenly, the Fletcher chief appeared, furious at the impudence of this stranger who had tethered his mount on Fletcher's land without permission.

Black Duncan knew that Fletcher had little English and was notoriously bad tempered. Words were exchanged; neither man understanding the other, swords were drawn and Campbell's servant, no match for the Fletcher chief, was killed.

Black Duncan suddenly appeared on the scene. Campbell told Fletcher that he would surely be hanged for murder and his castle and lands confiscated by the crown, but as a fellow-Highlander and neighbour, he would allow him to escape to France.

To protect Achallader from seizure, he convinced Fletcher to sign over his property to him and promised to hold it for him in trust until the furore died down and Fletcher could return and regain possession. Fletcher eventually came back from exile, but the property was never given back.

When the Fletchers lost Achallader, they removed the massive oak door from the front of the castle and carried it with them into history.

In 1976 we were invited by Col. Archie Fletcher, late Scots Guards, to visit him at his home in Glendaurel in Argyll, on the mainland not far from my mother's birthplace on the Isle of Bute.

We didn't know until we got to Glendaruel that Col. Archie's home was no ordinary house, but Dunans (from the Gaelic *dùnan,* little castle), one of the oldest, least known, and best preserved castles in the Scottish Highlands, and that Archie Fletcher was the laird.

While being shown around, we climbed a well-worn staircase which led up to the chapel. Although indoors and protected from the weather, the ancient oak door there was studded with iron bosses and appeared to have been exposed to the weather somewhere else and for a very long time.

An eerie feeling came over me. "Don't tell me" I said, "that you are of the same clan that left Achallader so long ago, and that that door is the same one your clansmen carried away with them from far Breadalbane?" "It is" said the Colonel, "my ancestors brought that door with them and placed it there to protect the sanctity of the chapel. A visiting priest says mass there for us from time to time."

Although Scotland has been mostly Presbyterian since the Reformation, there are still families in the Highlands that profess the Old Faith, the Fletchers of Dunans among them.

Glenelg, MacLeods And MacCrimmons

When a society or civilization perishes, one condition can always be found: they forgot where they came from - Carl Sandburg

Some of the people from Skye and Kintail in the Western Highlands of Scotland who came here two hundred years ago did not forget where they had come from nor where they had last set foot on their native land. They named the area in which they settled in Canada's Glengarry County after it. They called it Glenelg. Many years later the name was changed to Kirkhill. There are many Kirkhills in Scotland, but only one Glenelg.

The Scottish Glenelg, "the Glen of the Willows," is on the mainland near Knoydart, opposite the Isle of Skye on the Sound of Sleat. Because of its sheltered location, it was one of the few safe harbours for sailing ships on the windswept west coast of the Highlands.

Glenelg is only minutes away by boat from Kylerhea in Skye, but by land it is at the end of a long and dizzying road from Loch Duich in Kintail, the ancestral land of the MacKenzies and Macraes.

When Dr. Samuel Johnson and his biographer James Boswell passed over the Mam Ratagan Pass on their way to Glenelg in 1773, the eminent scholar almost lost his life when his horse stumbled on the precipitous and narrow track.

The road is wider now but still terrifying. The Highland bens are not nearly as high as the Rockies or the Alps but they can be even more forbidding at times. Highland roads are often single-track, which means that motorists have to remember where the last passing-place, marked with a white post, is situated. When an oncoming vehicle is met, the driver closest to a passing-place must pull off the road and wait while the other car, lorry, or bus squeezes past. Sometimes it seems that only a sheet of paper could be passed between the two. Sometimes it's even closer. In thick fog or storms, bumper to bumper confrontations are not unknown, frozen fear replacing the usual courtesies. It can seem like a Mexican stand-off in an old cowboy movie.

Glenelg was MacLeod of Skye land two hundred years ago. By the end of the 18th century many in the Highlands were prepared to leave their homes forever. Conditions had so deteriorated in the two generations after Culloden that emigration was not just a notion but a necessity. The deliberate destruction of the clan system which had held their Celtic society together for ages and the banning of the symbols of their culture — Highland dress, tartans, and weapons, coupled with government policies designed to destroy their fighting spirit produced a people who were demoralized and ground down.

This state of depression was particularly evident in the Western Highlands and Islands, which had supplied most of the support for the disastrous Jacobite Rising of 1745.

The "Bonnie Prince" who had inspired such loyalty and had led his Jacobite supporters to destruction had long gone and succeeding governments were determined to ensure that the Highlands would never again become the birthplace of rebellion.

The policy of "pacification" begun 30 years earlier after the 1715 Jacobite Rising was accelerated in 1746 and was so successful that no Highlanders after Culloden ever challenged the might of British power.

Military garrisons built throughout the Highlands with an occupying force designed to enforce government policy eventually were no longer needed. One of these garrisons, Bernera Barracks, was in Glenelg.

Although the MacLeods as a clan were not officially on the Jacobite side in the Rising of 1745, many MacLeod clansmen had strong Jacobite sympathies and defied their chief's orders not to join their fellow Highlanders. After Culloden it didn't make much difference in any case. Government retaliations fell heavily on all Highland people, often in spite of what side they had taken in 1745.

The MacCrimmons of Boreraig in Skye had been pipers to MacLeod of Dunvegan for centuries. Their college of piping fell into disuse by the end of the 18th century and the MacCrimmons themselves moved to Glenelg. A few years later many were in Canada, and it was generations before a MacCrimmon again played the music that had made Boreraig the centre of the piping world.

In Glengarry they found themselves surrounded by Gaelic-speaking neighbours, the troubles of the past gradually forgotten in the freedom of the Canadian wilderness. Boreraig Farm in Glengarry is still owned by McCrimmons, near the hamlet of McCrimmon and the Skye Road. Dunvegan is close by.

Some years ago Dr. John MacAskill, one of Scotland's finest pipers, came to Western Canada to teach the art of piping. He noticed that one of his students, whose last name he had not heard, was progressing much faster than the others. He always seemed to be one step ahead of everyone else. Dr. John told him to slow down. "Who do you think you are, sonny, one of the MacCrimmons?" teased MacAskill. "Yes sir," said the boy. "Don't get cheeky with me, boy!" said the doctor. "But that's my name sir.

I am a MacCrimmon." "Good Lord!" was the response, "I've never met a MacCrimmon in my life! I didn't think there were any left!" That young man became one of the greatest pipers in the world. His roots are in Glengarry, Ontario, and on the Isle of Skye in the Highlands of Scotland.

In 1793 an emigrant ship left Glenelg for Canada. On board were several hundred passengers, mostly MacLeods and their kin, but also including MacCuaigs, MacLores, MacDonells, MacGillivrays, Campbells, Fergusons, Grants, Murchisons, MacPhees, MacCrimmons and MacLennans, from Glenelg itself and neighbouring Skye, Kintail, Strathglass, Glen Moriston and Knoydart.

They were led by Kenneth MacLeod, a "gentleman of the clan" and his son Captain Alexander MacLeod.

They were not the first Highland people to settle in Glengarry but were typical of many 18th century arrivals.

The tacksmen who often led such groups to Glengarry were formerly the intermediaries between chief and clanspeople and were the first to realize that they had to leave to survive. These clan middle-men were generally well educated, could read and write, and spoke English and/or French as well as their native Gaelic. They were the ideal people to lead an emigration party and so it proved with what became known as the MacLeod Emigration of 1793-94.

Although the party had many misfortunes, had to return to port several times for repairs to the ship and had to spend the winter in Prince Edward Island, they survived under the care of their leaders and were able to take up land side by side in the area they called Glenelg in Glengarry when they finally arrived in 1794.

Some of their descendants live on the same land grants obtained two hundred years ago. On one of these farms on the Glenelg road, between Dalkeith and Laggan, the Clan MacLeod Society has erected a cairn commemorating the MacLeod Emigration. The farm has been in the George MacLeod family for over two centuries.

The early Highland emigrants who left before the Napoleonic Wars were the lucky ones. After Waterloo, the infamous Highland Clearances accelerated, but by that time Glengarry was a thriving community of Gaelic-speaking people, the memories of their Highland homes growing dimmer with each succeeding generation. They had found a new homeland.

In Scotland, Bernera Barracks in Glenelg is a ruin. The troops are long gone, as are the "wild hielandmen" who terrified them. A recent TV program featured a trip from the Australian Glenelg to Darwin. All the narrator could say about Glenelg was: "Glenelg, the place that's spelled backwards."

Campbells And MacDonalds

Murder under trust

Every so often we see a reference to the Massacre of Glencoe. There
was a sign put up in Williamstown here in Glengarry recently —
Remember Glencoe! — and some years ago my friend Rory MacDonald
put up a sign on his hotel in Glencoe, Scotland — *No tramps or Campbells
permitted.* Rory quickly took his sign down when he realized that it was a
poor joke and offended many people, not only Campbells.

But for how long should the terrible crime perpetrated on the
MacDonalds of Glencoe in 1692 be used against the Campbells, and were
they really guilty? Do all those bearing the proud Highland name Campbell
have to go through life continually being reminded of and insulted for
something with which they could not possibly have been involved unless
they had lived 300 years ago?

Neil MacNeill in his very entertaining little book *The Highland Heart
in Nova Scotia* tells a story about his uncle, a building contractor in Boston,
who fired a man on the spot when he learned that his name was Monteith.
"What did I do wrong?" the astounded man asked. "You betrayed William
Wallace!" said MacNeill. (Scotland's great patriot, as we all know from the
Academy Award-winning film, Braveheart, lived 800 years ago). And
MacNeill was still sore enough about this bit of ancient history to fire a val-
ued worker? This is nuts.

The facts about the Massacre of Glencoe are on record. We know the
names of those involved and how and why it happened.

The best book on the subject is John Prebble's *Glencoe.* It is essential
reading for anyone interested in Highland history. It forms a trilogy with
the same author's *Culloden* and *The Highland Clearances.* These three
books should be read by anyone interested in the true story of the Highland
Scots and why they came to Canada in such large numbers.

I'll try to summarize Prebble's Glencoe but I cannot do, in a few hundred words, what took Prebble three hundred pages. You'll have to read his
book to get the complete story.

It begins in 1689. William of Orange defeats James II of England (and
VII of Scotland), the last Stuart king to occupy the throne of Great Britain,
at the Battle of the Boyne in Ireland and James goes into exile.

Many Highland clans, called *Jacobites* after the Latin for James, are fiercely loyal to the Stuarts, whom they believe to be the legitimate heirs to the throne.

The new government knows that these clans are a threat to the peace and security of the country, and the clan chiefs are ordered to take an oath of allegiance to William before January 1, 1692. Some of the chiefs delay taking the oath before the deadline, including Cameron of Lochiel, MacDonell of Glengarry, and MacIain of Glencoe.

Sir John Dalrymple, the Earl of Stair and Secretary of State for Scotland, who hates Highlanders in general, puts forward a plan that he has been long preparing to crush the clans.

He is secretly pleased that some clan chiefs have not taken the oath. This gives him the opportunity to put his scheme into action.

Dalrymple is advised, and well advised, not to order an attack on the more powerful clans such as the MacDonells of Glengarry or the Camerons of Lochiel. But there is one clan that suits his purpose ideally: The MacDonalds of Glencoe.

In an area where clan feuds, cattle raids, and just plain bloody-mindedness are rampant, the small clan of the MacDonalds of Glencoe has one of the worst reputations of all.

They are feared and even hated by most of their neighbours. MacIain, the clan chief, has even been charged "with the slaughter of several people named MacDonald" and has escaped punishment. In 1689 the Glencoe men stripped the Campbell lands of Glenlyon from end to end, and not for the first time.

Dalrymple knows that few will come to their aid if they are attacked. He is right, and MacIain of Glencoe plays into his hands. He does not take the oath in time.

Robert Campbell of Glenlyon, a broken and embittered old man, is commanded to lead a company of the Earl of Argyll's Regiment into Glencoe and quarter them there to await further orders. Of Major Campbell's 68 troops, 10 are named Campbell.

After being hospitably received by the MacDonalds in their homes for two weeks, secret orders are received by Campbell in the name of King William of Orange:

> You are hereby ordered to fall upon the rebels, the MacDonalds of Glencoe, and to put all to the sword under seventy ... this is by the King's special command, for the good and safety of the country, that these miscreants be cut off root and branch.

And the orders are obeyed.

Clan feuds are a terrible part of Highland history. All clans are guilty of atrocities against rival clans and no race in history, ancient or modern, is free of blame for inhuman acts. But the Massacre of Glencoe is not a clan feud. It is murder under trust.

Glencoe is remembered not so much for the 43 slaughtered (200 escaped into the snow-covered mountains) but for the fact that it was done by men enjoying the hospitality of their victims.

The result of the horrible deed is as Dalrymple had hoped. The recalcitrant clans all bow to the new order. There is no rebellion in the Highlands for the next 25 years. But there is a reaction.

When news of the Massacre of Glencoe gets out, decent people throughout the British Isles and the continent of Europe are horrified. A Commission of Inquiry is formed to look into it. The conclusion is that those involved were only following orders.

Campbell of Glenlyon, although exonerated, is broken in mind and body. In drunken rages he would shout, "I would do it again — if the king gave me orders." In private, he says that he liked none of it. It is said by those who meet him in the streets and taverns of Edinburgh that "you may see Glencoe in his face." He dies ruined and a pauper.

His son and heir John Campbell fought on the side of the Jacobites in the Rising of 1715. MacDonell of Glengarry took his arm and asked to be accepted as a brother. MacDonell and Campbell charged the enemy side by side. In 1746 at Culloden, the same John Campbell, at the age of seventy, once again fought for the Stuart cause and against his own son who was an officer in the Black Watch. The old man died of exposure after the battle.

So what name should be reviled for Glencoe? Should every Campbell be blamed? Many Campbells are deeply hurt by the disparagement of their name. It is as good a name as any other and many of that name have achieved honour throughout history.

Should we blame anyone called Dalrymple? Or Duncanson, the officer who sent the fatal order on that day and boasted of it? Why should anyone be held responsible for the deeds of long-dead ancestors? *Mi-run mòr nan Gall,* the great hatred of the Lowlander for the Highlander, was the cause of much of the horrors of the past, and the Highlanders were not always blameless. But as the popular song *The Flower of Scotland* has it, "these things are past now, and in the past they must remain."

Here in Glengarry, except for the odd moronic crack about the Campbell-MacDonald feud, evidently meant to be hilariously funny, the Campbell name has always been respected. The truth is finally being recognized: The Massacre of Glencoe was planned and officially carried out by the government under orders signed by King William of Orange. Glencoe was just one of the many atrocities committed in the old struggle to extirpate the Gael.

Saint Patrick

Saint Patrick was a gintleman, he came of dacent people - Irish ballad

Saint Patrick's Day was once widely celebrated in Gaelic Scotland and was one of the major holy days — holidays — of the year, as was St Brigid's Day, St Michael's Day (Michaelmas), St John's Day and, of course, St Andrew's Day.

The name Patrick, in Scottish Gaelic *Padruig,* (pronounced Pah-rug), is from the Latin Patricius, an aristocrat. St Patrick was not born in Ireland. He is traditionally considered to have been the son of a Roman father and a Celtic mother of noble ancestry although there is much that is not known about his origins. Some authorities think that he was born in Scotland — Roman Caledonia — where his father was a soldier serving in one of the outposts of the Roman Empire along the Antonine Wall which was erected to keep out the "Wild Caledonians" from Roman-occupied southern Scotland.

The Romans never penetrated very deeply into the Scottish Highlands. Garrisons, such as the one at Fortingall in Breadalbane, were under almost constant attack from the native tribes and had to be gradually abandoned as the Roman Empire collapsed.

The Rev. Dr. Patrick O'Regan of St Finnan's Church in Glenfinnan told me in 1951 that his research had convinced him that Patrick was born "over the hill" in the Lochaber area sometime in the 4th century. The details of his life will probably never be known for sure, but it is generally believed that Patrick was captured by pirates as a youth and sold into slavery in Ireland. He eventually escaped, left Ireland, became a priest, and was then drawn irresistibly back to the land of his enslavement as a Christian missionary.

Patrick's name was eventually so revered among the Irish that for a thousand years after his death his name was seldom used in baptism, and few were named after him. It was only after the death of Patrick Sarsfield, the great Anglo-Irish Protestant hero of the 17th century that Patrick became a common name in Ireland.

In Scotland, the name Patrick, sometimes in the diminutive form Para or confused with Peter, was and still is fairly common. Killfeather, Gaelic *Cill-Phadair,* is rendered in English as both St Peter's or St Patrick's Church. It has been said that in the Highlands the first-name Patrick is the Sunday name and Peter the everyday one.

Among the first to put bagpipe music into notation two centuries ago were two ministers, the Rev. Patrick and his brother the Rev. Joseph Mac-Donald, and Patrick was a favourite name among the MacCrimmons, MacLeods, Lamonts, and MacGregors, as well. MacPatrick, *Mac-Phadruig,* is a rare family name but is common in the anglicized forms Patterson, Paterson, and Pattison.

If Ireland's great St Patrick was born in Scotland, it seems only fair that Scotland's great St Columba of Iona, *Colum-Cille,* was born in Ireland. Of course, this was long before Scotland was called Scotland and long before there was any concept of nationalism as we know it today. The people of early Ireland and Scotland were united by a common language and culture and felt themselves simply part of the Gaelic world. The divisions were to come much later which eventually caused many Scottish Gaels to believe that they had little or no connection with the Irish Gaels, and vice-versa.

In Ireland, St Patrick's Day is celebrated, of course, as a national holiday, but more as a religious observance and in a more dignified way than in other lands where the Irish have settled. Irish-born people seeing the St Patrick's celebrations for the first time in places like New York or Boston are often amazed, if not horrified, by the celebrations surrounding the memory of their national saint. But at least these are joyous celebrations; they do not commemorate any battles or massacres and everyone, Irish and non-Irish, joins in having a good time.

It would be an improvement if more authentic Irish music was played at these celebrations and less bogus Tin-Pan Alley stuff, but things are improving with the popularity now of groups like The Chieftains, Clannad, and shows like Riverdance. But please, it's not Paddy's Day. We don't call the English patron saint Georgie or Scotland's saint Andy, so how about extending the same courtesy to St Patrick? He deserves it.

Samuel Johnson in the Highlands

I am always sorry when any language is lost, because languages are the pedigree of nations — Dr. Samuel Johnson

It pains me to hear all of Scotland's woes blamed on the English. Certainly there was much animosity between the two nations from the earliest times as there was bound to be when two distinct peoples occupied the same island and one was so much more powerful than the other. But for the Gaelic-speaking Highland Scots their enemies were often closer to home.

For over eight hundred years the non-Gaelic Scots, the Lowlanders, consistently showed a strong and continuing antipathy to their Highland neighbours. The feeling was mutual. The Lowlanders seemed to believe that the Highlanders were uncouth and violent savages, bent on robbing them, and the Highlanders often obliged by acting accordingly. The Highlanders seemed to believe that the Lowlanders were scheming, ignorant outsiders, bent on stealing their land, and the Lowlanders often proved them right.

It was only when writers like Samuel Johnson in the late 18th century reported what he had witnessed, and Sir Walter Scott in the 19th presented the Highlander as a romantic hero that public opinion beyond the Highlands changed. The exploits of the Highland regiments, Queen Victoria's love for her favorite castle of Balmoral and her affection for what she considered the Highland way of life enshrined the transition.

There is a persistent rumour that Victoria wished to effect a reconciliation with her Celtic subjects by establishing a residence in Ireland but saner minds prevailed and her gesture was directed to the more amenable Highland Celts. There were much fewer of them — the population of the Highlands was about 300,000 in 1850 compared to over 8 million in Ireland. And they were about 90% Protestant, the suspect Catholics mostly removed overseas after Culloden.

Although largely bogus, the picture of the Highlander as a tartan-covered, well-behaved North Briton continues to this day. But the actual condition of the people of the Highlands during Victoria's reign was little different from that of their Irish cousins.

Attempts to expose the true state and identity of the Highland Scots and in particular to preserve the Gaelic language and heritage that distinguishes them have too often been met with suspicion, if not outright hostility.

The English have generally shown a bemused indifference to what they sometimes perceived as the peculiarities of the Scots. Any ambitions to extend England's borders into Scotland expired in the 17th century, and in any case, the remote and unproductive Highlands never much excited the interest or envy of England.

Dr. Samuel Johnson, the personification of the High Church Tory Englishman and the compiler of one of the first dictionaries of the English language, loved to make fun of the Scots, often at the expense of his friend and biographer, the Lowland Scot James Boswell. But Johnson was a great Moralist, as that term was understood in the 18th century, and throughout his life felt obliged to speak out when he encountered injustice.

In 1773, when he and Boswell travelled with great difficulty to the Highlands, they kept separate records of the trip. Johnson's was published as *Journey to the Western Islands of Scotland* and Boswell's as *Journal of a Tour to the Hebrides With Samuel Johnson, LL.D.*

As they soon discovered, the people were already leaving. Johnson wanted to learn more about the Highland Scots and was horrified at what had happened to them after the defeat of Culloden twenty-three years before. He wrote what no Scotsman had dared to write. Of the thousands of Highlanders who were serving in the British forces the world over, some "pressed" into service, some serving only to ensure their families' safety, he wrote:

> Thus England has for several years been filled with the achievements of seventy thousand Highlanders . . . Those that went to the American war, went to destruction. Of the old Highland regiment, [the Black Watch] consisting of twelve hundred, only seventy-six survived to see their country again.

The figure of 70,000 Highlanders in the British army may be an exaggeration, but the figures for the Black Watch are substantially correct.

Johnson hated to see the Highlands losing the proud race that had lived there for a thousand years:

> There seems now, whatever the cause, to be through a great part of the Highlands a general discontent. That adherence, which was lately professed by every man to the chief of his name, has now little prevalence; and he that cannot live as he desires at home, listens to the tale of fortunate islands, and happy regions, where every man may have land of his own, and eat the product of his labor without a superior — whole neighbourhoods form parties for removal, so that departure from their native country is no longer exile. He that goes thus accompanied, carries with him all that

makes life pleasant. He sits down . . . surrounded by his kindred and his friends; they carry with them their language, their opinions, their popular songs and hereditary merriment; they change nothing but the place of their abode; and of that change they perceive the benefit.

Johnson made emigration sound like a pleasant adventure and of course he knew nothing of the hardships of pioneer life in the Canadian wilderness, but his words eventually proved true. Thus were Highland communities like Cape Breton and Glengarry founded.

When Samuel Johnson visited the Highlands with Boswell long before travelling to this remote area had become popular or even practical, they suffered great difficulties. There were few roads or inns, Johnson was old, corpulent, gouty and often bad-tempered, but he persevered. He and Boswell had planned their trip for many years. When Boswell visited the French philosopher Voltaire in 1764 he told him of their plans to visit the Highlands. "He looked at me as if I had talked of going to the North Pole and said, 'You do not insist on my accompanying you?' — 'No sir.' 'Then I am very willing you should go'. "

As it happened, Johnson and Boswell visited those very areas of the Highlands — Kintail, Glenelg, Skye, and some of the Inner Hebrides from which many of the early settlers to Glengarry were to come shortly after. Indeed, many of them were already making plans to leave for Canada and the Carolinas. Perhaps some of the Macraes and MacLeods that Boswell and Johnson met *did* eventually come to Glengarry.

On the mainland near Skye Johnson and Boswell stayed with a man called McQueen. Johnson was impressed by the fact that McQueen had built a substantial house with his own hands and had a library. Boswell reported:

> After dinner, Mr. McQueen sat with us a while.... He said, all the Laird of Glenmoriston's people [the Grants] would bleed for him, if they were well used; but that 70 men had gone out of the Glen to America. That he himself intended to go next year; for that the rent of his farm, which 20 years ago was only five pounds, was now raised to 20 pounds... that he could pay 10 pounds, and live, but no more. Dr. Johnson said, he wished McQueen laird of Glenmoriston and the laird to go to America. McQueen answered, he should be sorry for it; for the laird could not shift for himself in America as he could do.

Johnson has often been thought of as being anti-Scottish. As an English High-Church Tory he was not sympathetic to the Lowland Scots and enjoyed teasing his Lowland companion Boswell at every opportunity. But with the Highland Scots it was quite a different story. He knew that there was something of great antiquity and beauty to be found among the people of the Highlands and he was not disappointed.

He first heard the Gaelic language in an Inn at Nairn, near Inverness. As Boswell reported:

> Over the room where we sat, a girl was spinning wool with a great wheel, and singing an Erse [Gaelic] song. 'I'll warrant you,' said Dr. Johnson, 'one of the songs of Ossian.'

This incident was featured recently on the CBC radio program Ideas, from Toronto. Joanne McKenna, who sang Gaelic songs here in Glengarry as a child, played the part of the Highland girl.

Johnson did not like what had happened to the Highland people after 1746. He was particularly critical of the cruelties imposed on them by many of their former chiefs. Boswell quoted him:

> Were I a chief, he said, I would dress my servants better than myself, and knock a fellow down if he looked saucy to a MacDonald in rags; but I would not treat men as brutes.

MacKenzie of Seaforth and the Macraes

Sgur Urain! A mountain in Kintail - the War Cry of Clan Macrae

The Macraes were traditional allies and supporters of the MacKenzies. For their loyalty to the MacKenzie chief they were known as MacKenzie's Coat of Mail. If it seems strange that the "rae" in Macrae is not capitalized (although it is not that important) it is because, unlike most Highland names which honour some illustrious ancestor, Macrae means "son of grace," possibly a religious reference, or perhaps "son of fortune," a more romantic derivation. The name is spelled *Macrath* in Gaelic, pronounced Macraw. It is the same name as the Irish McGrath or McGraw, but not necessarily connected.

Duncan MacPherson in his book *Gateway to Skye,* written some 50 years ago, describes the fate of the Macraes of Kintail after the Napoleonic

Wars. The Seaforth referred to was the Earl of Seaforth, the MacKenzie chief who, like so many of his contemporaries, was seen by many Highlanders as betraying his own clan during the years after the defeat of Culloden. He has no descendants.

> It is difficult to understand why the Highlanders, a proud race ever ready to fight, suffered so tamely during the Highland Clearances. The usual procedure was for the landowner (the laird or chief) to spend most of his time - and what money he could extort from his tenants - carousing in London or Paris. In these haunts, where he was, in all probability, looked upon as a simple barbarian, he was readily fleeced. So the cry for more money came back to the Highlands. The miserable hirelings who were left in charge of the estates drained the people of every penny they possessed and then proceeded to evict them. The land could be put to more profitable use. Naturally the government did not bother about the plight of men they did not require, for the wars were over for the time being and there was no immediate need for soldiers. They had never heard the old Gaelic saying: 'Where there are no boys in arms, there will be no armed men.' So the evictions went on; then, when the glens were deserted, the government woke up. They appointed a Royal Commission!

MacPherson goes on to tell the true story of what happened to the people of Kintail when the landlords discovered that sheep were more profitable than humans. It is not a unique story; it was repeated over and over again throughout the Highlands. It must be remembered, though, that many of the chiefs and landowners were themselves suffering from great financial difficulties, and most were torn between losing everything and the only other alternative they had; making their land profitable. Many also sincerely believed that the land could no longer support a large population and that their clanspeople would be better off in Canada or Australia. That would eventually be true, but to the people of the glens at the time of the evictions the thought of being forced out was not a happy one.

> Seaforth evicted a large number of tenants from the lands of Kintail. His factor, Duncan Mór Macrae, carried out the evictions - and added much of the land to his own extensive sheep farm. Men of his own clan were rendered homeless; they were driven into exile to satisfy the greed of their callous kinsman and their selfish chief. Men and women, young children and the aged, all were driven from their homes. Perhaps the most bitter pang of all was the realization that their chief, for whom they would have given

their lives, had no further use for them. All he wanted was money, and they had none to give. Taking with them their scanty possessions, they crossed the Atlantic in filthy boats, herded like cattle. After enduring great hardship [some] finally settled at Glengarry in Canada. In that hospitable land they prospered, and their descendants live there today, a thriving community. But what of the factor and his chief? 'The laird is bad enough,' says the old proverb, 'but the factor is the devil himself.' Alas for Duncan Mór Macrae's schemes! He died penniless and ruined. As for Seaforth, he was obliged to sell his inheritance and the last of his race has passed on.

So Duncan MacPherson wrote in 1939. The first Highlanders who came to this country at the end of the 1700s were generally better off than those who came after Waterloo. Those first settlers were either disbanded soldiers with their families, such as those who came up from the Mohawk Valley in New York, or groups under the leadership of a tacksman or other respected person, such as those who sailed from Glenelg in 1793, or the MacMillan settlers who came in 1802.

No people leave their native land, their relatives and friends and the graves of their ancestors willingly. Even if they were not forced out bodily as were the later victims of the Clearances, they were forced out in other, more subtle ways.

Is it any wonder that even with the hardships they suffered in the early days in Glengarry, they developed such a strong love for Canada? Here there were no chiefs to betray them and they could own their own land. When we came here 25 years ago we bought a Macrae farm. We called it Kintail.

The Road to Glenfinnan and St Finnan's

The remembrance of things past — Shakespeare

We left Glen Nevis and drove by Loch Eil, through Fassifern to St Finnan's Church. All familiar names here in Glengarry. But we weren't in Canada . . . we were in Scotland.

This road from Fort William at the foot of Ben Nevis to the sea at Mallaig opposite the Isle of Skye has echoed to the tramp of marching men for a thousand years and more.

Vikings moored their longboats on the coast and travelled inland on this road to terrorize the Gaels in the tenth century; the Lord of the Isles and fighting men of Clan Donald left their Hebridean kingdom three hundred years later and followed the same road inland in a vain attempt to conquer the Scottish mainland; in August, 1745, Bonnie Prince Charlie led his cheering Jacobites down this same road to victory after victory until their final devastating defeat eight months later at Culloden, and along this same road in 1746 came the British troops that were to punish the Highlanders with fire and sword, and disgrace the name of British justice; and it was along this road, and others like it, that the dispossessed people of the Highlands struggled with their meager belongings to board the ships that were to take them from their native land forever.

This is Lochaber, and the lament played so often at Highland funerals around the world encapsulates the anguish of those exiles in three words: It is called Lochaber no More.

Glen Nevis is behind the Lochaber town of Fort William, at the foot of Ben Nevis, the highest mountain in Britain. It is a short distance off the main road, and like many Highland glens, it is a dead-end. You can drive in and out, but not through. I mention it because it is one of the many place-names that were brought here to Glengarry with the early settlers. Glen Nevis in Scotland is now a favourite spot for hill walkers or for those who want to climb Ben Nevis. It is one of the most beautiful glens in the Highlands, and was once the home ground of the MacSorlies, a senior branch of the Camerons of Lochiel.

Years ago there was a book written about a bar in New York titled *McSorley's Wonderful Saloon*. I assumed at the time that McSorley was an Irishman. Maybe he was, at least in the author's mind. The name derives from the Gaelic pronunciation of Somerled, the part-Norse, part-Celtic progenitor of Clan Donald in the 12th century. But before Somerled became a personal name, it was Norse for a summer raider or Viking, so perhaps there are MacSorlies in Ireland, because the Vikings raided there too. What we do know for sure is that the Cameron MacSorlies are long gone as a clan from Glen Nevis in Scotland. Perhaps some came here to Glengarry. Perhaps some of the Camerons here were originally MacSorlies.

Fort William is an ideal centre for exploring the Western Highlands. It is the only town in Lochaber, and many of the place-names in the area were brought to Canada by the early settlers; Glen Garry, Laggan, Glen Roy, and the places on the road to Glenfinnan. Glencoe is close by.

Fort William was originally called *Cille Mhoire* (Keelya Vurrah - St Mary's Church) or Maryburgh in English. Later it was known as *An Gaireasdan*, The Garrison, when the government stationed soldiers there to police the Highlands, and finally it became Fort William. Many visitors from Canada find it convenient to stay there when exploring the land of their ancestors.

After leaving Fort William the road to the west passes along the shores of Loch Eil. The word *eil* may come from the Gaelic *iall* meaning "cattle" but it is very old Gaelic and we don't know for sure. The chief of Clan Cameron is always titled "Lochiel," spelled for some reason that way, with the *e* and *i* reversed. When Gaelic names are rendered into English they are sometimes spelled in strange ways.

Fassifern, mid way along Loch Eil, is spelled Fassfern on the road-sign there. It means "the Alder Grove," *Am Fasadh Fearna*. It was there Bonnie Prince Charlie spent the night as the guest of Cameron of Fassifern after the Royal Standard was raised at Glenfinnan on August 19th, 1745, marking the beginning of the Jacobite Rising which promised so much and which ended the following April in the mud and blood of Culloden.

Prince Charles Edward Stuart has been portrayed as a romantic hero, but his ill-advised attempt to place his exiled father on the throne of Great Britain was doomed from the start and resulted in the deaths and suffering of thousands of Highland people and the eventual destruction of their way of life.

The only aspect of Bonnie Prince Charlie's life that merits admiration was his behaviour during the many months that he wandered the Highland hills with a few loyal supporters after the defeat of Culloden. As a young man of 25, he endured great hardship with courage and good humour, earning the love and respect of all those with whom he came in contact.

But he eventually escaped to France and oblivion, leaving his Highland people to pay the price exacted by a victorious government; their homes, furnishings and crops burned, their livestock driven off, and many of those who were not executed or imprisoned left to starve.

Even those who had taken no part in the Rising and who had no Jacobite sympathies were often punished as well, their names and Gaelic language enough to identify and condemn them. The government was determined to make sure that the Highland Scots would never again cause any trouble.

The policy of "pacification" would eventually result in the removal by force or economic necessity of thousands of families and the turning of the Highlands into a wasteland. The English intellectual Dr. Samuel Johnson who toured the Highlands twenty-seven years after Culloden and saw what had happened to the people perhaps said it best:

To hinder insurrection by driving away the people, and to govern peaceably, by having no subjects, is an expedient that argues no great profundity. . . where there was formerly an insurrection, there is now a wilderness.

A few miles after Fassfern, we turn a corner and there it is — Glenfinnan, and the towering memorial to the Highlanders who lost so much because of their loyalty to the man they believed was born to be king.

Bernie MacCulloch of Glen Roy, the Glengarry historian who has often helped me with information for these columns, was speaking to me one day about the preservation of the St Raphael's ruins here. He's one of the founders of *The Friends of the Ruins Inc.*, the group formed to preserve the walls of the burned-out church. "Isn't it about thirty years since you started that Glenfinnan Association to save St Finnan's church in the Highlands?" he asked.

Bernie was right. It had slipped my mind, because for some years now St Finnan's in Glenfinnan has been looked after by a group in Scotland formed to protect and repair historic churches, regardless of religious affiliation, and St Finnan's was one of the first on the list. Now we know that it will be safe forever.

When I first travelled to the Scottish Highlands in 1951, I was 19 years old. I spent my first few days in Glasgow with family and friends and then set off for my mother's birthplace, the Isle of Bute. Rothesay, the main port and town, was a holiday resort much favoured by Glaswegians who annually sailed "doon the watter" to spend their vacations on the Firth of Clyde islands of Bute or Arran or on the mainland of Argyll or Ayr.

My grandfather was the landlord of *The Grapes and Vines* in Rothesay and attended to the needs of the hard-drinking male holidaymakers while their wives and children dabbled their toes in the cold Atlantic waters along the shore. Although the front of the island was typical of any holiday resort on the Clyde, the back of the island showed a more traditional face. Gaelic was still heard on some of the farms as it was on the pier at Rothesay when I first went there.

My mother had advised me to call on an old family friend, an expert on the history, language, and traditions of the Highlands. Canon Andrew Butler was living in retirement in a small cottage at Ascog, near Rothesay. In 1911 he had conducted the burial service for my grandfather and had kept in touch with the family ever since.

I spent many happy hours with him, listening to his tales of a lifetime spent ministering to those in the Diocese of Argyll and the Isles. He had received his higher education in Douai near Paris and spoke fluent French as well as Gaelic. During the 1939-45 War many Polish servicemen in exile were stationed in Scotland and Canon Butler also learned Polish so that he could minister to them.

He was also an expert on the poetry of Robert Burns and often included apt quotations from Scotland's national bard in the many letters that he sent us.

I visited him several more times on other trips to Scotland and the memory of those happy days will remain with me always.

Canon Butler gave me the names of many people in the Highlands who would help me with information. One was Dr. Patrick O'Regan of St Mary's and St Finnan's in Glenfinnan. "He may appear a geographical misfit," said the Canon, "but he's a fine fellow and his mother was a Clanranald MacDonald. He claims that St Patrick was born on the other side of the hill from Glenfinnan. Perhaps he's right, but nobody else seems to agree with him."

When I got to Glenfinnan I called on Fr. O'Regan. He was indeed a fine, gentle man, although a bit of an absent-minded professor. When I saw the sad state of his church, designed by the famed English Victorian architect Pugin and one of the most beautiful of its type in Britain, (contemporary with the present St Finnan's Cathedral here in Alexandria), I was upset. I suggested that if some of the Canadian MacDonalds whose ancestors came from the area knew that this historic church needed repairs, they might be glad to help. He was not enthusiastic.

When I returned several years later, his successor, Fr. Joseph Campbell, jumped at the idea. "Go to it, boy!" he said.

On my return to Montreal I contacted some MacDonald friends and the Glenfinnan Association was born. During the next fifteen years we collected enough money to fix the roof and walls, install electricity and heating, and keep the church from further deterioration. By the time we finished, the Glenfinnan Association had a membership of over 100, including many non-Catholics.

Anyone visiting Glenfinnan should visit the church, a five-minute walk from the visitors' centre. It is a sight worth remembering, with a magnificent view from the front door down Loch Shiel. On a misty day you can almost see the unfortunate Bonnie Prince Charlie coming in to shore with his doomed supporters two hundred and fifty years ago.

Some historians believe that the Royal Standard was not raised on that day in August, 1745 where the present column was erected, but on the hill where the church now stands.

Apart from the Montreal Glenfinnan Association, another connection with Canada at Glenfinnan is the visitors' centre and gift shop there. It was financed by the late David Stewart of the Macdonald Tobacco Company in memory of Sir William Christopher Macdonald, the founder of the firm and one of Canada's greatest philanthropists. Sir William was the grandson of Capt. John Macdonald of Glenfinnan and Glenaladale, MacDonald of the Glens, who led his people to Prince Edward Island in 1772. He was the last of the old-style clan chieftains. His grandson William, though destined for the priesthood, changed his mind and became one of the richest men in Canada instead.

The MacNeils, Barra, and the Coddy

A visit to the Outer Hebrides

The MacNeils are a rather small clan, both here in Glengarry and in Scotland. There are more MacNeils in Canada and in Cape Breton particularly than there have ever been on their ancestral Hebridean Island of Barra. After seeing the 1949 hit movie *Whisky Galore* (re-titled *Tight Little Island* for North American audiences) Anne and I were determined to visit Barra, the scene of the film, on our honeymoon in 1954.

In an old schedule I found in Scotland on a subsequent trip many years ago dated 1906, the boat for the Isle of Barra left Oban at 6 a.m. daily. That's the time it left when we sailed there in 1954 and I suppose it will still be leaving at the same time in 2054. Some things don't seem to change much in the Highlands and Islands.

Anne and I arrived on the pier at Oban at 5 a.m. and asked the attendant there what we should do with our car. "Chust leave it there," he said. "How long will you be away on Barra?" "About a week," I said. "Fine, fine. Your car will still be there when you return." And so it was. There was no charge for parking then, but I'm sure that's all changed now.

We carried our luggage aboard in the bright morning sun. It was early in the month of June and in the North of Scotland at that time of year it scarcely gets dark at night. We were as far north as Bergen in Norway or James Bay in Canada.

We set sail and soon left Oban Bay behind. Within a short time, or so it seemed, we were passing Duart Castle, the home of the MacLean chief on the Isle of Mull.

Then came Tobermory, the principal town on Mull, where one of the galleons of the Spanish Armada sank 400 years ago. There was a crew of Navy divers there working on locating the wreck. A rumour had persisted that a fortune in gold was on the ship when it sank, and the owner of that part of Mull, the Duke of Argyll, was sponsoring the underwater search. "There's no treasure on that ship," said one of the crewmen on the ferry as we tied up at the dock in Tobermory. "The MacLeans got it off and safe away a long time ago."

Months later, back in Canada, we read in the papers that nothing of importance had been found on the wreck by the latest treasure hunters.

After leaving Tobermory, we had a kind of a meal on board and then went up on deck to enjoy the view of the Outer Hebrides on the horizon.

Early in the afternoon we spotted Ben Heaval, the highest point on Barra and an hour or so later we landed on the pier at Castlebay. Kishmul Castle, the ancient home of the MacNeil chiefs, sits on a little rocky islet nearby. It was being restored by a wealthy American MacNeil who had been recognized by the Lord Lyon, King of Arms, as the MacNeil chief. (A farmer in Prince Edward Island probably had a better claim to the chiefship, but he was not interested).

There was certainly no monetary advantage to becoming the MacNeil chief. The wealth of the clan (if there had ever been any) had long gone and the new chief, an architect, was spending his personal fortune rebuilding the little castle. And there it stands today, thanks to him.

The people of Barra were not very enthusiastic about their new chief. They had managed for generations without any official chief and held no romantic illusions about a way of life long gone. The new chief spoke with an American accent, had no Gaelic, and did not share the religious faith of the people of Barra.

They took great delight in telling us of the first visit of the 45th chief to the island. The entire population was crowded onto the pier in their best Sunday clothes, the children in front, the adults behind. MacNeil started down the gangplank, splendidly adorned in his new kilt from Anderson's in Edinburgh, the three eagle feathers of a chief waving in his bonnet. He graciously acknowledged the cheers of the crowd, and then the children began to sing! What a surprise! He had not expected such a tumultuous welcome. Then he noticed something odd. No one was looking at him. Their eyes were on someone directly behind him. Kenneth Grant, the Bishop of Argyll and the Isles, was arriving to administer the sacrament of confirmation to the children.

Barra is a small island and the population never exceeded a thousand or two, but in olden times MacNeil of Barra considered himself the equal of any monarch. Each evening, after the chief and his family had dined, his herald would climb to the topmost rampart of Kishmul Castle and shout to the four corners of the world, in Gaelic, "MacNeil of Barra has had his dinner. The other kings and princes of the world may now dine."

Barra is remembered in modern times for the motion picture that brought us to the island. *Whisky Galore* was based on the book by Sir Compton MacKenzie about a true incident which occurred during the Second World War. A ship carrying a cargo of whisky bound for the U.S. foundered off the Isle of Eriskay near Barra. To the Hebrideans, who had had their supplies of "the water of life" severely restricted due to wartime rationing, such a catastrophe seemed like manna from heaven.

Much was made in the movie of the necessity of the islanders to wait until the end of the Sabbath before they dared set out to liberate the whisky. It made a good story: The strict Presbyterians standing unhappily on the shore all day Sunday, staring out at the wreck teetering on the rocks and waiting for the clock to strike midnight. But Barra is a Catholic island, and although their faith discourages servile work on Sunday, exceptions are made in the case of emergencies. As one old fellow told us "as soon as the Sunday service was over, we headed out to the wreck. Surely it was a matter of necessity to save the cargo before it went to the bottom of the sea!"

The people of Barra, Eriskay, and South Uist were able to get a great deal of the cargo off the ship before it finally sank. We saw the outline of the wreck once when we were crossing in a small boat from Eriskay to South Uist. "It caused the most excitement since Bonnie Prince Charlie landed here in 1745," said a woman on Eriskay. As most of the bottles were hidden by men in a very emotional and tired state who forgot the next day where they had buried their loot, the plough still turns up a few bottles from time to time. "I hope that the ones still buried have cork tops" a man said to us on the boat to Barra, "the metal ones are bad. They rust through in no time at all."

At the time of the shipwreck, the great Pipe-Major William Ross, head of the Army School of Piping in Edinburgh Castle, received a cable from his friend John MacPherson, "the uncrowned king of Barra," known better by his nickname "Coddy." The message, subject to strict wartime censorship, read: "You played well on the wireless last night, my friend. Come and visit us as soon as possible. You will receive the freedom of the island as you have in the past. The cows are calving, the hens are laying, small mercies are coming in from the sea, and there is nothing here but politics." Willie was on the next boat out of Oban. He knew that there were no elections pending in Barra, but he also knew that the name of the sunken whisky ship was the Politician!

I once had the temerity to ask the Coddy where he got his nickname. He gave me a sort of "fish-eye" and said that he couldn't really say. I understood his reticence when I looked up my Dwelly's Gaelic Dictionary and found that the word that sounded most like Coddy was "codag", a haddock. When Anne and I first met John MacPherson over 40 years ago, he was a distinguished old gentleman, a little below medum height, with a white moustache and bright, intelligent eyes. He had a rather long face in proportion to his body and I suppose you could imagine his schoolmates, many years ago, tacking the "coddy" moniker on him. In any case, he was quite proud of it.

His old friend Willie Ross often visited the Coddy when teaching piping to the young people on Barra, Eriskay, and South Uist, and these islands produced many fine pipers. This area had never suffered the persecution of their music as had many other places in the Highlands and Willie enjoyed the enthusiasm for piping among the young people there.

One year he arrived to find his star pupil absent from the class. "Where is Alasdair MacKellaig?" he asked. A little boy piped up. "He's away, Pipe Major." "Away where?" said Willie. "Away to Blairs College in Aberdeen," he was told. "And why is he going to this Blairs College?" fumed the great man. "To learn to be a priest," came the subdued answer. Willie was not of a religious nature. "What a (expletive deleted) waste of a good piper!" said Willie.

Seumas MacNeill, professor at Glasgow University and co-founder of the College of Piping, was a native of Glasgow, not Barra, but he once said that South Uist and Barra were the only places in the world where you could hear a woman humming a pibroch while wheeling a baby carriage.

But to return to the legend of the 1941 bonanza that visited the Barra area in the form of a shipload of whisky: The topsoil in the Hebrides is very thin and seaweed is carried up from the shore to enrich the ground in the small fields so that potatoes can be grown. The year after the Politician went down, Willie Ross was once again a guest of the Coddy. At the evening meal, Willie remarked on the small size of the potatoes. "They're only about the size of big peas, Coddy" said Willie. "Oh well," said his host, "you can't have it both ways. There's only a few inches on top to grow them, and then the bottles start!"

The Coddy liked to tell the story of the man (not himself, of course — his stories were always about "some fellow") who tried to hide bottles from the wreck down a rabbit warren. "Every time the fellow pushed a bottle down a hole it would come clunk up against another one already there. He finally gave up and just sat down and drank up all he had. It took him three days."

Unlike the film *Whisky Galore*, where no one was caught, in real life several men were arrested for illegal possession of spirits and brought to trial in the courthouse at Lochmaddy, North Uist. A few were convicted, but one man was let off due to the ingenuity of his lawyer. "Isn't it a shame," the barrister said, "that a man can be tried in a language that he does not understand!" The English-speaking judge let him off. Finlay MacKenzie, the proprietor of the Lochboisdale Hotel in South Uist, who told us the story, finished with the punchline: "Of course, the accused could speak perfect English, but the judge didn't know that!"

The legend of the Polly whisky lives on. Many a tourist is duped into buying, as a souvenir and for a premium price, a "genuine" bottle, suitably antiqued, that has arrived legitimately from the mainland the day before. A recent article from the London Times reported that the last authentic bottles from the famous Politician were sold at one of London's largest auction houses for an incredible amount. A teetotaler is always at an advantage.

The Lady of Lawers

Hear the voice of the Bard! Who present, past, and future sees!
— William Blake

Lawers is about ten miles east of what many consider the loveliest village in the Highlands, Killin, in the district known as Breadalbane. Many of the early settlers here in Glengarry came from that area, including the MacEwens, some Campbells, MacLaurins, MacLores (MacLures), Dewars, MacGregors, and MacNabs.

The Lady of Lawers lived over 300 years ago. She was a seer, someone who seemed to have the ability to see into the future, an ability she shared with many others throughout Scottish history.

In olden times, many areas had people who, from time to time, could predict coming events. Most of them and their auguries would have been known only to those in their immediate neighbourhoods and long forgotten, but the Lady of Lawers was different. All of her many predictions except three have come true, the last one as recently as 1948.

Breadalbane, *Bràghad-Albainn* in the original Gaelic, means "the breast (or breadth) of Scotland." It is a vast area that stretches from the Eastern Highlands of Perthshire to Loch Awe in Argyll. Grant Campbell QC named his home near Williamstown "Kilchurn Castle," (pronounced *Killya-hurran*), because it was from the castle of that name in Scotland that the Campbells of Glenorchy had spread eastwards. By the end of the 17th century, the first Earl of Breadalbane could boast that he could ride in a straight line for 100 miles and never be off his land.

It is believed that the Lady of Lawers was a Stewart of Appin who marrried a Campbell of Breadalbane and came as a bride to Lawers on Loch Tay about 1650.

One of her early prophecies concerned a new church that was being built there. "The ridge stones will never be placed on the roof" she said. "If they are, then all my words are false." Everyone scoffed at her strange prediction, but when the carved sandstone capping stones were unloaded and piled on the shore of Loch Tay, a violent storm arose in the night and washed them into the loch. They could not be recovered and some can still be seen half-buried in the sand in deep water. Different materials were used to finish the church.

After her weird prediction about the church stones came true, the Lady of Lawers was listened to with more respect. Very few could read or write Gaelic in those days, so the oral tradition was the means of passing on anything of importance. The ability of the early Celts to memorize vast amounts of knowledge was recorded with amazement by the Romans when they conquered Gaul and ancient Britain.

Auguries from someone as famous as the Lady of Lawers would have been remembered word for word in Breadalbane and beyond. They were taken seriously and often referred to people and places that were easily identified. It was very important to those who believed such things to recognize the omens and portents the Lady foretold so that the results could be avoided if possible. The trouble was that no one knew just when her predictions might come true.

Actually, few of the Lady's prophecies actually came true in her lifetime, which was probably very lucky for her. In an age of great superstition and cruelty, she may have been burned at the stake as a witch if her predictions had been considered the work of the devil or if they had offended someone in authority.

In Ross-shire, far to the north of Breadalbane, at about the same period, Kenneth MacKenzie, the Brahan Seer, was said to have been boiled in oil by Lady Seaforth because he had reluctantly told her that her husband was cavorting with another woman far from home.

One of the Lady's better-known prophecies was "the jaw of the sheep will drive the plough from the ground." It came true over a hundred years after her death when the Lowland sheep were brought in by the landlords to displace the people, resulting in the infamous Highland Clearances. Another of her prophecies also referred to depopulation: "The land will be sifted and riddled of its people."

The second Marquess of Breadalbane started clearing his lands of people in 1834. The last Marquess left his ruined estates forever in 1948. The Lady of Lawers had predicted that the last of his line would ride out of Breadalbane on a pony. Whether he knew of the augury and had a strange desire to fulfil it or whether it was just a coincidence, he rode his favourite pony over the hills and away forever on that sad day.

Today there are less than 100 people living on Lochtayside, where there had once been thousands. Another of the Lady's sad prophesies has come true: "The homesteads on Loch Tay will be so far apart that a cock will not hear its neighbour crow."

Knoydarc

We'll take leave of Morar, / Arisaig, and mountainous Moidart, / Eigg, and fair, surf-swept Canna, / and beautiful, lovely Uist — Anna Gillis

Donald Simon Fraser of the Lochinvar Road reminded me recently that I should always give the original Gaelic spelling of a place, with the pronunciation in phonetics and the meaning of the word in English. This is easier said than done, because phonetics are purely a personal choice; Gaelic is a very old language and has many subtle sounds that are unknown in English and difficult to render into phonetics. For instance, Donald is *Domhnall,* and you would have to hear a Gaelic-speaker pronounce it to get it right. The closest I can get to it is Daw-ull, the first syllable rather nasal and the second very short, but someone else may prefer different phonetics.

As far as meanings are concerned, Gaelic is such an ancient language that some words or phrases are too old or obscure to translate easily.

Knoydart as it is now written in English is pronounced Noy-dert, the stress, as always in Gaelic, on the first syllable. But in Gaelic it is *Cnoideart,* and it is devilishly difficult in English: Kron-dyarsht is the nearest I can get to the proper sound. Knoydart is a special place name here in Glengarry because so many of the first settlers came from there.

Donald Fraser has a good knowledge of Gaelic, and says that he always knew the area east of Dalkeith as *Cnoideart,* but didn't connect it with Knoydart until he heard Gordon MacLennan, the Gaelic scholar, pronounce it in Gaelic and in English when he visited Glengarry about 20 years ago. And no wonder Donald was confused! The Gaelic and the English versions are so different that they sound like two different words.

As to the original meaning, I don't really know. It is very old Gaelic and could mean "hilly," from the Gaelic *cnoc,* a hill or high place. If that is so, it is well named, because Knoydart is one of the most mountainous areas in the Highlands of Scotland. It is inaccessible by road and can only be reached by boat, by walking for miles over the neighbouring hills, or by helicopter.

The easiest way to see Knoydart from a distance is from the south end of the Isle of Skye. From there you can view it as it has been since the beginning of time, although in prehistoric times the Highland hills were forested and are now bare, except for areas that have been planted with trees during the last hundred years. Nothing, certainly, has changed since the people left for Canada two centuries ago.

The population of Knoydart never exceeded a few thousand, although it is a huge area of about 400 square miles. But it is almost all vertical; the people lived on a narrow strip along about 100 miles of shoreline between the ocean and the mountains, and in a few glens deep in the hills.

I have referred often in these articles to the English word *Highland* as a misnomer for the Gaelic people who lived there. Although it has become an accepted term and I gladly use it in the title of my column and in my writing, most people in the Highlands lived (and still live) in the valleys or the low-lying areas, often just a little above sea level. Those are the only areas that can be cultivated, except for a few plateaus in the central Highlands large enough to provide arable land.

The only reasons that anyone would have to climb the mountainous slopes would be to bring cattle to the upland meadows for grazing in summer, (and then they would stay in temporary shelters called *shielings*), or for hunting game. Most permanent dwellings and townships were (and still are) in the lower and less exposed areas.

In the Scottish Knoydart, as far as I know, there is no one left who is directly connected with the people who lived there 200 years ago. The entire original population is long gone, the first ones coming here to Glengarry at the end of the 18th century.

Among those early exiles to Canada were some of the MacDonells of Scottas, the MacDonalds of Croulin, and of Sandaig, the Sandfields and many more from the 30 or so tacks or little townships that dotted the Knoydart peninsula. Those who didn't come here are scattered the world over. Those that were left were eventually cleared by a succession of land-lords in the 19th century. Those few who live there today are descended from people who moved in later.

The first settlers in Glengarry, along with others from the Scottish Glen Garry, Lochaber, Kintail, Glenelg, Skye, and Breadalbane, were joined by others over the years from the same general areas. They provided the lead-ers that helped build Canada. They gave the lie to the calumny that Scot-land was better off without them. The truth is that the Highlands never recovered from their loss.

There was a Scottish TV series a few years ago shown on TV Ontario called *The Munro Show*. (A munro is a mountain over 3,000 feet, named for the man who first climbed all 200 of them in the Highlands). On the show, a different mountain was climbed each week. One of the programmes featured Knoydart, where, we were told, it took the climbers two days just to get to the mountain they were scheduled to climb. Scenes of Knoydart were shot from a helicopter and they were awesome and mag-nificent. It was truly another world. The only thing missing from the glens shown on TV was people. There were none.

Halloween

From ghoulies and ghosties and long-leggety beasties / And things that go bump in the night, Good Lord deliver us! Anon.

It is hard to believe that it is only within living memory that Halloween has become a celebration observed by non-Celtic people. Originally a pre-Christian ritual in Ireland and Scotland called *Samhuinn* (pronounced Sah-win), it marked the beginning of the Celtic year. The second part of the year began with the celebration of *Beltane* (May 1). *Samhuinn* was celebrated on Nov. 1.

The non-Celtic peoples divided the year according to the solstices, the shortest and longest days of the year. When Christian missionaries first be-gan converting the Celts, it was their policy to graft a Christian feast or holy day onto a day that was already held sacred by the people, so *Samhuinn* be-came All Hallows Eve, or Halloween, for the Celts, as Yule became Christ-mas for the Nordic people.

Most of the non-religious aspects of our Christmas come from the Germanic people. The Celts preferred to celebrate Christmas as a purely sacred day and to reserve their whooping and hollering for Halloween, and, later on, for New Year's Eve.

Samhuinn was the original Thanksgiving Day for the Celts. The harvest was in and the people prepared for winter, observing the end of one year and the beginning of another. The fact that November marked the apparent death of most growing things led to the ancient Cult of the Dead, when the spirits of the deceased came back to revisit their homes.

It is easy to see how the Christian festival of All Saints, commemorating the "blessed dead," fitted in with the old Celtic celebration. And that word "old" might refer to two thousand years ago or to fifty years ago. It all depends on where you're talking about and to whom.

Alec McDonald, the retired farmer from Lochiel who now lives in Alexandria, said to me one day that he enjoyed reading my columns but when I wrote of second-sight or ghosts he found the subject ridiculous. "I don't believe all that nonsense," he said, and then proceeded to tell me all about the time, years before, that they had heard shuffling steps in the attic and the sliding of what sounded like a large box across the floor. The next day they heard that a neighbour had died. "That was the ghosts getting the coffin ready," he explained.

It's not so long ago that things like that happened in the Highlands too. F. Marian McNeill in her book *Halloween* tells the story of how one of her friends was mistaken for a ghost. It happened on the Hebridean island of Barra early in this century. He was a painter who was spending some time sketching the seascapes that surround the little island, and found himself there at Halloween time.

Even 50 years later, when Anne and I stayed on Barra and Eriskay, visitors were rare and tourists just about unknown. The old ways had not yet completely died out and if you were trusted and accepted into the community, you would sometimes be privileged to hear stories that would not ordinarily be told to outsiders and be included in some of their activities.

Such was evidently the case with Marian McNeill's artist friend, John Duncan. On Halloween, some of the local boys asked him to help them make masks, as there were none that year in the only store on the island. He somehow obtained a large roll of cotton, cut out coverings for the head, painted them with what he thought were funny expressions, and handed them out, keeping one for himself.

The first house they called on was full of people. When the door opened, there were screams of fear and some of the women threw themselves on the ground in terror. They lifted the masks, and everyone roared with laughter. Then, in Duncan's own words, written down at Marian McNeill's request, the plot thickened:

> After visiting several houses with similar effects, the lads said: 'Let's visit uncle Eachann!' Now uncle Eachann was a great big fellow over six feet tall. He had the reputation of being the strongest man on the island and also the most superstitious. He lived all alone in a black house on the other side of the island. 'He will murder us,' one of the lads whispered to me reassuringly.
>
> As we approached the lonely house, everybody tip-toed silently. They shoved me to the front, knocked at the door and drew to the side. I felt like a sacrificial victim. I faced sudden and violent death. Old Eachann shuffled to the door. Before I could say a word, he took me by the right hand and with deference and courtesy led me to the fire, set me on the bench and sat down beside me. We sat thus in silence. I thought to myself, 'it's all up. He knows me well enough,' and I lifted my mask to speak to him. He gave a violent start and shrank from me. I said, 'did you not know me?' and my blood was frozen, in turn, when he stammered, 'I - thought - you - were - a - dead - man!'

Loch Arkaig

'Twas I that led the Highland host / Through wild Lochaber's snows / What time the plaided clans came down / To battle with Montrose
— Aytoun

Eileen and Jim Seay are two strong supporters of The Glengarry Highland Society. They often give me information that I can use in this column and in the Heritage classes at Glengarry District High School. In the summer of 1994 they went on the "Return to Lochaber" tour to Scotland. These tours have been organized on a regular basis for many years by Dr. Hugh P. MacMillan, with Prof. Ted Cowan, former Head of the School of Scottish Studies at Guelph University, as tour guide.

Other Glengarrians on the '94 tour were Edie and Donald McCrimmon of Glen Norman, who never miss an opportunity to go on these popular trips. Eileen has loaned me the video of their holiday. It will provide me with lots of material for future use. I am very grateful to the Seays and to all those readers of *Highland Paths* who send me items that I may be able to use in future columns.

On the Seays' video there is some beautiful footage taken around Loch Arkaig in Lochaber, a part of the Highlands seldom visited by outsiders. It lies just south of Glen Garry (two words there). As they say over there, it "marches" with the ancient lands of the MacDonells of Glen Garry to the north and east and the MacDonalds of Clanranald to the west.

The Loch Arkaig area is the home of the Highland MacMillans (there is another branch of the family in the Lowlands) and marks the northern border of the lands of the Camerons of Locheil, with whom these MacMillans were allied. It was also the home of Archibald MacMillan of Murlaggan, (there is another Murlaggan in the MacDonald of Keppoch country) and his cousin Allan of Glen Pean, who led the Lochaber emigration to Glengarry in 1802, the subject of the recent book *The Lochaber Emigrants to Glengarry.*

There were other names in Lochaber, of course, besides Cameron and MacMillan, such as MacPhee, Kennedy, Grant, Stewart, MacArthur, MacLean and MacDonell, but in the days of clanship they would have followed whatever clan ruled in the area in which they lived, regardless of name.

Before cash money became the usual medium of exchange, rent was paid through shares of produce, usually livestock and grain, which went to the tacksmen, the agents of the chief, and in service to that chief in the clan regiment. No Highland chief could tolerate disloyalty among his people, for obvious reasons, so if you wanted to hold on to your little patch of land, you followed the rules or were thrown out.

Long before the terrible clearances of the 19th century, the practice of clearing individuals and families from clan territories by the chiefs sometimes occurred for various reasons, not always justly. The fate of those cleared could result in destitution and death, for no other clan would readily take in the dispossessed, and they were sometimes reduced to wandering the roads and begging for their bread. It is thought that that is the origin of the tinkers, the native gypsies who still wander throughout Scotland and Ireland.

The true gypsies came from the east, spoke their own language called Romany and dealt mostly in horses, while the tinkers often spoke Gaelic and specialized in repairing pots and pans. Their caravans can still be seen on the roads and their distinctive round green tents in the fields of sympathetic farmers and landowners.

In 1746 a large sum of money destined for the Jacobites was sent from France but arrived too late to be of any use. Some say that it was buried near Loch Arkaig and is still there. Others think that "the Loch Arkaig treasure" was spirited away a long time ago. In any case, the real treasure of Loch Arkaig, the people, have all gone and are dispersed throughout the world with the other "children of tempest," the exiled Highland people who found other loyalties in other lands.

Boat People

Fair these broad meads, these hoary woods are grand
But we are exiles from our fathers' land — Canadian Boat Song

At Feis-Glengarry we try to keep everyone smiling. It is a joyous thing to celebrate the Highland heritage of Glengarry and a *feis* (pro."faysh") is a feast or a festival, so why bring up unhappy memories? If sad things happened "long ago and far away" let's forget them and get on with our lives. It serves no purpose to dwell on the past, unless it's to make sure that the mistakes of the past are not repeated. As George Santayana wrote in his Life of Reason, "Those who cannot remember the past are condemned to fulfil it."

That is why we presented our Glenelg Pageant at the Feis in '94 — not to wallow in the suffering of people forced to leave their native land and to undergo the pain of an ocean crossing, but to show the strength and bravery of those unsung heroes who built a new Glengarry. To pretend that an emigration across the ocean was a happy excursion, like a modern-day holiday cruise, is to demean the truth.

The beautiful and uplifting results of the tribulations of these "boat people" as portrayed in the Pageant were the kindness and generosity they received in Canada, and the help and support that those who came before gave to them.

The first settlers from the Highlands of Scotland who came to Canada would never have survived if they had not been helped by the Native people and by those who had preceded them across the seas. To understand how important the conditions in the New World were to those early arrivals, when government assistance was virtually unknown, and when everyone had to fend for themselves, we have to understand what tribulations the people suffered before they even got here. What few of the first settlers ever described were the terrible conditions on most emigrant ships.

While some of the earlier immigrants from the Highlands may have had some cash to afford a degree of comfort not enjoyed by later victims of the Highland Clearances, sailing across the Atlantic for people who had never before been to sea could be horrific.

Here is what James Hunter says in his recent book *A Dance Called America:*

> Highland emigrants had always run some risk at sea. Of the two hundred or so people who embarked on the brig Nancy, which sailed from the Dornoch Firth in September 1773, for example, only about a hundred stepped ashore, nearly three months later, in New York. The remainder, including all but one of the fifty-one children under the age of four, had died in the course of a voyage made at an especially hazardous time of year on a ship where passengers were expected to get by on "corrupted" water and musty, rotting oatmeal said to be "hardly fit for swine."

Hunter describes how timber-carrying cargo ships were temporarily converted to passenger vessels to make the return trip to Canada profitable:

> Here, [in the hold] in a space which was usually so confined as to make it difficult for an adult to stand up straight, there were then constructed two tiers of roughly built wooden berths, one such tier running along each side of the vessel, with a third being placed amidships on occasion. Each of the dozens of berths which were thus provided measured some six feet by six. Each of these berths — the higher one some 24 or 30 inches above the lower — was intended to hold a minimum of four people, with emigrants of both sexes and all ages being bundled together in conditions which are utterly beyond our modern imagining.

Conditions were not always as horrible on emigrant ships as they must have been on the brig Nancy. Capt. John MacDonald to St John's Island (P.E.I) in 1772, Capt. Alexander MacLeod in 1794 and Archibald MacMillan in 1802 to Glengarry were enlightened leaders who sincerely helped and protected those under their care on the trip across the ocean. But even at the best of times, it was no picnic, and first-class accommodation was only for a very few. There are those who believe that "cleanliness is next to godliness" and cannot accept that their forebears were anything

but well-dressed, well-scrubbed, and well-off. As the young people say today, "get real."

Sons of Scotland Society at McCrimmon, Sept. 1st, 1900.
[Photo courtesy of Glengarry Pioneer Museum, Dunvegan, Ontario]

The New Land

The Ticonderoga Vision

It's a far cry to Loch Awe — said by Campbells when in another country

Near the north end of Loch Awe in the Western Highlands of Scotland stands Inverawe House. There, some two hundred and fifty years ago, a story began to unfold that if true, remains one of the strangest examples of second-sight ever recorded.

The tale has been passed down in the Campbell family involved from generation to generation and referred to by such eminent historians and writers as Francis Parkman and Robert Louis Stevenson. This is an excerpt from Dean Stanley's version, endorsed by the family of the man himself:

> Late one evening, as the laird, Duncan Campbell, sat alone in the old hall, there was a loud knocking at the door. Opening it, he saw a stranger, with torn clothing and kilt besmeared with blood, who in a breathless voice begged for asylum. He went on to say that he had killed a man in a fray, and that the pursuers were at his heels. Campbell promised to shelter him. 'Swear on your dirk!' said the stranger; and Campbell swore.

The dirk or dagger was worn suspended from the waist. The taking of an oath on iron was considered unbreakable from the most ancient times. If a sword was used, the blade was grasped near the handle, the hilt and blade forming a Christian cross, thus making such an oath doubly sacred.

> He then led him to a secret recess in the depths of the castle. Scarcely was he hidden when again there was a loud knocking at the gate and two armed men appeared. 'Your cousin Donald has been murdered, and we are looking for the murderer!' Campbell, remembering his oath, professed to have no knowledge of the fugitive; and the men went on their way.

> The laird, in great agitation, lay down to rest in a large dark room where at length he fell asleep. Waking suddenly in bewilderment and terror, he saw the ghost of the murdered Donald standing by his bedside, and heard a hollow voice pronounce the words: 'Inverawe! Inverawe! blood has been shed. Shield not the murderer.'

In the morning Campbell went to the hiding place of the guilty man and told him that he could harbor him no longer. 'You have sworn on your dirk' he replied and the laird of Inverawe, greatly perplexed and troubled, made a compromise between conflicting duties, promised not to betray his guest, led him to the neighbouring mountain and hid him in a cave.

The mountain behind Inverawe House is *Ben Cruachan*, which looms large in the lore of the Campbells of Argyll. It was on the slopes of this mountain that the progenitor of the clan, the legendary Diarmid, was reputed to have killed a wild boar single-handedly. The crest of the Campbells is a boar's head, and their war cry is *Cruachan*.

In the next night, as he lay tossing in feverish slumbers, the same stern voice awoke him; the ghost of his cousin Donald stood again at his bedside, and again he heard the same appalling words: 'Inverawe! Inverawe! blood has been shed. Shield not the murderer!'

At break of day he hastened, in strange agitation, to the cave, but it was empty; the stranger had gone. At night, as he strove again to sleep, the vision appeared once more, ghastly pale, but less stern of aspect than before. 'Farewell, Inverawe!' it said; 'farewell till we meet — at Ticonderoga!'

For years, Duncan Campbell tried to find out what Ticonderoga meant or where it was located. No one at that time had ever heard of it. When Campbell, as a major in the Black Watch, met veterans of campaigns in Africa or India, he would ask them if they knew of such a place, but to no avail.

His regiment was eventually sent to America and one day in 1758 as they were marching along the shore of Lake Champlain in what is now New York State, he asked the Mohawk guide: "What is that point of land called that I see in the distance?" "The French call it Carillon, said the guide, "but we call it Ticonderoga." "Then that is where I will die" said Campbell.

In the Union Cemetery between Sandy Hill and Fort Edward, New York, a gravestone bears this inscription: "Here Lyes the body of Duncan Campbell of Inverawe, Esqr, Major of The Old Highland Regiment aged 55 years who died the 17th July, 1758, of wounds he received in the attack of the retrenchments of Ticonderoga or Carillon, 8th July, 1758."

Gaelic Faces

Where's the face one would meet in every place? — Keats

In The Glengarry Connection section of the December/January '92-'93 edition of the Halifax publication *The Clansman* there is a column about Gordon MacLeod of Dunvegan.

In the article, Gordon tells of the time that he and some others from Glengarry were visiting Cape Breton and were taken for locals by a man in Mabou because of their accents when speaking English. After seeing the photo that accompanied the article, I would suggest that it wasn't only their accents that caused the man to think that they were Cape Bretonners. Anyone from Glengarry travelling through Cape Breton or the Scottish Highlands would observe the same thing—the people often look like our relatives. And that is only natural, because many *are* our relatives.

The Highland world is a rather small world. We often think, because of the influence of the Highland Scots throughout the globe, that there must have been a great number of them. There was not. In ancient times most of Scotland was Celtic and Gaelic-speaking and about 90% of the place-names in Scotland are of Gaelic origin, but by the end of the 1700s when the first settlers came here, Highland Scots were in the minority in Scotland.

The total population of the Highlands never exceeded about 300,000, the Lowland or non-Gaelic population continually expanding from a minority in the Middle Ages to about five million, and Gaelic-speakers shrinking to about 2% of the total today.

Of course, there are a large number of Gaels living beyond the Highlands, but they generally became identified with the non Gaelic world, except in places like Cape Breton and Glengarry, where the language continued to be spoken for many generations. This is all the more striking when we realize that our fellow-Gaels in Ireland were largely still Gaelic speaking until well into the 1840s, when the population there was close to 8 million, but there never were Irish speaking settlements comparable to Cape Breton or Glengarry outside of Ireland.

The Irish, like others who settled in Canada, came as individuals or in small family groups. Only in the case of the Highland Scots did entire communities come together to the New World, bringing their language and local traditions with them and often settling side by side, changing little except their place of abode.

The Scots Highland influence on the music of the world is quite remarkable when we consider that Highland Gaels were largely isolated from the mainstream European musical tradition and, until the violin was introduced, their music (apart from the voice) was based mainly on only two instruments — the harp and the pipes.

Much of the music of Lowland Scotland can be traced to Gaelic sources and even the Irish music of Donegal and Antrim has been influenced by the music of the Scottish Gael. The opposite is also true, but not to the extent that one would expect from a population 30 times greater than Gaelic Scotland. Which brings us right back to the small Highland world and the faces that go with it.

If the man in Cape Breton thought that Gordon MacLeod and company were Cape Bretonners because of their accents, their faces would have helped as well. There are many families in Glengarry and Nova Scotia who have only Highland names in their pedigrees as far back as they can trace them. In many clans facial characteristics are passed on, so that we can sometimes say "that is a MacLeod face" or "he has a real Highland nose."

The famous portrait of Kenneth MacKay, the Cameron Highlanders' piper whose playing helped turn the tide of battle at Waterloo, shows a face that is almost the double of a Superior Court judge who lived in Montreal a few years ago whose name is the same, although there is no direct connection.

This story from Lindsay Cameron, advertising manager of The Glengarry News in Alexandria, Ontario, illustrates this in an uncanny way. He swears that it is true, so if you don' t believe it, take it up with him. I'm only the messenger.

Lindsay's uncle, John Cameron, had been overseas with the famed 401 City of Westmount Fighter Squadron during the last war. Some years after his return to Canada he was sent by his employer, an electrical contractor, to supervise the installation of electricity in a cheese factory in Williamstown.

As he walked into the place for the first time, he noticed some men taking a break. He nodded at them and then, recognizing a familiar face among them, went over and shook the fellow's hand. "Long time no see," he said, "I'll have a chat with you later." After the day's work was done, he returned to talk to his friend. "Now where did I see you last?" he said, "I can't quite remember." The other man, it turned out, had also been overseas during the war, but in the infantry. As they compared notes on where they might have come in contact, they realized that they had never met. "Well anyhow," Lindsay's uncle laughed, "my name is John Cameron." "So's mine" said the stranger.

New Year in the Highlands

An old tradition honoured

Là, (pronounced "lah") is the Gaelic for "day." There were many special days in the Scottish Highlands in olden times, several of which were brought to this country 200 years ago and honoured as long as Gaelic was spoken. Gradually the English versions replaced some of them and others were simply forgotten.

Among the most important were *Là fhéill Brighde* (Lah fail Breeduh), St Brigid's Feast Day: *Là Bealltuinn* (Lah Bee-ail-tun), May Day: *Là fhéill Micheil* (Lah fail Mee-hull), Michaelmas: *Là fhéill Eòin* (Lah fail Yowen), St John's Day, and *Là Muire* (Lah Moor), St Mary's Day. The Virgin Mary was never called *Màiri* in Gaelic but had her own special name *Muire*, reserved for her alone. A complete list of these days can be found in *Dwelly's Gaelic-English Dictionary*.

Là Bliadhn' ùire (Lah Blee-ahn oor), New Year's Day, is in a class by itself. The Scots, both Highland and Lowland, and the French celebrated New Year's Day in grand style. Gifts were exchanged, visits to friends and relatives took place and every home was an "open house."

Sometimes if New Year's Eve had been celebrated not wisely but too well and with all the hospitality handed out on the day itself remarkable scenes often occurred. This tradition is still carried out in military messes across the land and in a much more dignified manner at the Governor General's levée in Ottawa.

Although all of Scotland celebrated New Year's Eve, *Hogmanay* to the Lowlanders, *Oidhch Challuin* (uheek-yuh hall-een) to the Gaels, there was a special ceremony performed in the Highlands and remembered by many here in Glengarry. It generally took place on New Year's Eve. It was called *dol air bhonnaig,* (going out on the bonnach.) A bonnach or bannag is a flat sort of cake made from oatmeal or barley meal and cooked on a griddle or in an upright position before an open fire. The Native people of Canada call homemade bread bannoch because of their contacts with the early Highland fur traders.

Dol air bhonnaig began with a visit by a group of men to every home in the community. Each house was circled three times from east to west, *deiseil* (dyash-al), the way of the sun. This movement from east to west, probably pre-Christian, was observed for many rituals and ceremonies, from treating disease to setting out on a trip by land or sea.

After circling a house, the men knocked at the door. It was considered good luck to have the darkest man enter first. One of the men carried a sheep's skin or large piece of leather on his back which the others struck it with sticks as they circled the house three times on the inside.

The man being struck wept and wailed and those striking him kept up a barrage of words describing the ills of the past year. The idea was that all the bad luck and evil of the previous year would be knocked out on his back.

Once the ceremony was over, the men were offered food and drink and a special New Year's bonnach which they would put in a basket or bag. If there were many houses to visit, the hospitality might catch up with them and cause some problems, but the poorest home in the community always received the collected bonnachs.

The late Angus Hoey McDonell, columnist in *The Glengarry News* for 70 years, often mentioned the ceremony and our neighbour Gilbert MacRae told me he remembered it well. From what I can make out, the tradition gradually died out here, except for the visits and the liquid donations which were consumed on the spot to avoid spillage. Annoyed wives and the temperance movement put the finishing touches to it. The Highland Society would like to revive the custom, using ginger ale instead of spirits, but something tells me that it would never achieve the popularity of the original.

A Glengarry New Year's Eve

An old tradition revived

On the evening of December 31st, 1993, the Glengarry Gaelic Choir gathered at Kintail Farm to bring in the new year. The old Highland custom of "going out on the bonnach," still remembered in Glengarry, was celebrated.

Just before midnight most of us went outside and circled the house from east to west three times, following the pre-Christian Celtic tradition honouring the path of the sun, called *deiseil* in Gaelic.

It was no easy walk in the bitter cold and deep snow, but all survived.

Then the darkest man knocked loudly at the door and asked admittance. Once inside, I was selected to carry a sheepskin on my back while the others armed themselves with sticks and thumped me with them while we circled around the kitchen and parlour, symbolically knocking out the evils of the past year. I was glad to have the protection of the sheepskin.

When the hilarity was over, a Gaelic prayer was recited by the guests, asking for a blessing on the house and all those within it and wishing everyone health and happiness for the coming year.

The head of the house, my wife Anne, presented us with the biggest and hardest oatmeal bonnach ever made, thanks to choir member Lorna Chapman. It will be good for many years to come. It may not have been edible, but it was a fine symbol, representing the oatcakes that were collected on New Year's Eve and presented to those in need.

The Gaelic New Year's Eve, *Oidhche Challuin*, pronounced "Uheek-yuh-halleen" was traditionally celebrated with variations on this theme. In some areas the ceremony was performed on Christmas Eve and called *Oidhche nam Bannag.*

After we sang the best known song in the world, Robert Burns' *Auld Lang Syne,* (no, that's not Gaelic; it's *Lallans,* the other language of Scotland, and means "Old Long Ago") the Lowland ceremony of first-footing was performed, courtesy of Fiona Fraser and husband Stanley.

Both Highland and Lowland traditions require a dark man to be the first to enter the house in the new year. Stanley went outside when no one was looking and knocked long and hard at the door until it was opened. He threw some coins in first to signify hope for prosperity, a piece of coal to represent warmth, and a bottle of Scotch for either joy or sadness, depending on your point of view.

In typical Glengarry style we then joined choir member Bob Lemieux and wife Denise in singing a French New Year song. It was a real Canadian party.

The Gaelic Choir sang into the wee hours, interspersed with instrumental music by Darrell MacLeod, Dave McCormick, and Gerald Rory McGillis.

As most of the choir and guests seemed to be teetotallers, the only aspect of a Scottish-Canadian New Year's Eve celebration missing was the traditional hilarity associated with broken heads, broken furniture, broken hearts and broken promises. That part wasn't missed.

Clan names

Clanna nan Gaidheal ri guaillibh a chèile -
Children (clans) of the Gaels shoulder to shoulder —
Rallying cry of the Highlanders

Since these columns are about the Highland background of Glengarry, clan names here mean Gaelic names, and Gaelic names can sometimes be puzzling. Most last names were originally spelled quite differently from the modern English forms that are familiar to most non-Gaelic speakers, and exactly *how* they are spelled now can often lead to arguments.

Everyone is proud and possessive of the name he or she bears. To suggest that the same name may be spelled in many ways is only asking for trouble, although even some members of the same family may spell the family name differently, and not only in Gaelic. There are several versions of Shakespeare's name, all signed by him. But in his day people didn't worry much about spelling. There were few serious dictionaries of the English language until over a century after Shakespeare died. Before that time, words were spelled as they sounded to the writer and nobody much cared.

How we spell our names is surely our business, but now that spelling has long been standardized, variations can only be explained by the preference, in preceding generations, for a different orthography or by a misunderstanding such as occurred so often in ships' passenger lists, or by a deliberate change in spelling to make a name more exclusive.

In English, the most usual last name is Smith, as in blacksmith, gunsmith, silversmith or any other kind of smith. A smith is a craftsman, and if your family spelling is Smythe or Psmith, that is your business, but a smith is still a smith.

The big problem with Gaelic names (and all names beginning with Mc or Mac are Gaelic) is that they were often spelled by people who did not speak the language, or if they did, could not write it. It was an oral culture and the written language was known to only a few.

In the Gaelic tradition, you are known by your *sloinneadh* or patronymic, a list of your ancestors, such as the poet Angus MacDonald of Glencoe, *Aonghas Mac Alasdair Ruaidh,* Angus, son of Red Alexander. If a person was well-known, such as a poet or illustrious leader, the last name was seldom used because everyone knew it.

The listing of ancestors could include dozens of names, particularly in the case of the aristocracy, where succession was important. The children of clan chiefs had to learn their patronymics by rote, going back hundreds of years. Some clans carried ancestry back to ridiculous extremes, such as the MacNeills of Barra, who claimed direct descent from the daughter of the pharoah of Egypt after whom the Nile was named!

In England, the use of last names dates back to the Domesday Book, ordered by William the Conqueror in 1086, although it referred only to the aristocracy. It did not apply, of course, to the Kingdom of Scotland, but the Anglo-Norman custom of adopting permanent last names gradually spread to that independent country as well, at least among the non-Gaelic population. The Highland Gaels already had their own system of family names, and looked down on anyone who could not recite a long line of forebears.

Even today, many people of Highland extraction find it difficult to understand how anyone could not know the names of their grandparents. That is one of the reasons why an interest in genealogy has become such a popular study.

If you think from the foregoing that family or clan names were always sacred, think again. Undoubtedly Gaelic people took great pride in their names, but there were exceptions. If your name was out of favour, for one reason or another, or outlawed as in the case of the MacGregors, you might be forced to adopt another. Rob Roy MacGregor signed a letter, on display at Inverary Castle, asking help from his kinsman, the Duke of Argyll. He signed it "Rob Roy Campbell."

The story is told of Sir Walter Scott, on a visit to the Highlands, being introduced to a local man. "But I met you some years ago" said Scott, "and that was not your name then." "No," said the man, "but that was when I lived on the other side of the hill!"

In the days of clan warfare, it was sometimes unwise to bear the name of the wrong clan in enemy territory. To a people who revered ancestry, survival meant more.

As is so often the case with the Celts, things are not always as they seem. Most clan names, it is true, derive from some famous progenitor, often long forgotten, but some are simply trade names, such as Macintyre, *Mac an t-saoir,* son of the carpenter, or MacGowan, *MacGhobhainn,* son of the smith. Many are ecclesiastical, dating from the old Celtic church when priests could marry - MacTaggart, *Mac an t-sagairt,* the son of the priest, MacNab, *Mac an aba,* the son of the abbott, or MacMillan, *MacMhaolain,* the son of the tonsured one or monk. This last name shows how confusing it can be when a Gaelic name, which really can only be spelled properly one way in Gaelic, can be massacred by those who do not know how to write Gaelic. There are over one hundred and fifty different English spellings of MacMillan.

Another Celtic confusion occurs when nick-names become family names. A perfect example is the name Campbell. *Caim - beul* means crooked mouth, originally applied to some forgotten ancestor. The chief of Clan Campbell, the Duke of Argyll, is always called *Mac Cailein Mór* in Gaelic, the son of Great Colin, another ancient hero, but before the nick-name Campbell became official, the clan was known as *Sliochd Dhiarmaid,* the race of Diarmaid, and so individuals were known as MacDermid, *MacDiarmaid,* or any of the various forms of the name such as MacDermot, and there are still many of that name in Argyll.

It is wise not to get too dogmatic about how Highland names are spelled in languages other than Gaelic. Outside the Gaelic world, anything goes. So *MacDhomhnuill* becomes MacDonald or MacDonell or any of dozens of variations, including Maldonado in Spanish or Magdonelle in France or Belgium. In areas where so many have the same last name, the clan name is often taken for granted.

Strange Things

Time present and time past / Are both perhaps present in time future /
And time future contained in time past. — T.S. Eliot

The Highlands have always had seers, those people who seemed to be able to see into the future. Even the Irish Gaels recognized this ability in some of their Scottish cousins. In MacBeth, Shakespeare has the three witches foretelling what good or evil will befall the unfortunate king. Although he was not aware at first hand of the Gaelic way of life, Shakespeare knew that second sight was a well-known attribute of some Scots.

The seer was usually uncomfortable with this strange ability, never seeking to have it known except to a few and only reluctantly prophesying when pushed to it.

The Highland seer, unlike the fortune-teller, never sought out those to whom prophesies may have referred and never accepted any form of payment. Often the gift of second sight was considered a curse by those who possessed it.

We all know of things that cannot be explained logically, such as thinking about someone, perhaps for the first time in ages, and suddenly getting a phone call from that very person. Life is full of such coincidences. Is there such a thing as extra-sensory perception? The modern world does not seem to be the place for it. We prefer rational explanations for what our ancestors thought of as sorcery.

The man known as the Brahan Seer, Kenneth MacKenzie, was known in Gaelic as *Coinneach Odhar,* Pale Kenneth. There is some doubt as to his identity, but he was possibly a farm labourer at the MacKenzie castle of Brahan in Ross-shire in the 17th century. According to legend he received the gift of prophecy as a child. He fondled a small smooth stone when he was foretelling the future. Many of his predictions have been passed down by word of mouth for almost four hundred years. Some of them have come true, some of them have not . . . or not as yet!

The Countess of Seaforth supposedly prevailed upon him to tell her what her husband was doing while away from home. The seer tried to avoid telling her of his vision, but, against his will, had to reveal that he saw her husband involved in some hanky-panky in Paris. For his trouble, the enraged Countess had the seer executed. Before he died he uttered his most famous prophecy:

> I foresee the doom of the House of Seaforth. I see a chief, the last of his line, and he is both deaf and dumb. He will be father to four fine sons, but he will follow them all to the grave. He will live in sorrow and die in mourning, knowing that the honours of his line are extinct and that no MacKenzie will ever again rule in Kintail. The last of his possessions shall be inherited by a widow from the east who will kill her own sister. As a sign that these things are coming to pass there will be four great lairds in the days of the last Seaforth: MacKenzie of Gairloch shall be hare-lipped, Chisholm of Strathglass shall be buck-toothed, Grant of Glenmoriston shall be a stammerer and MacLeod of Raasay shall be simple-minded. These four chiefs shall be allies and neighbours of the last Seaforth and when he looks around him and sees them he will know that his race has come to an end.

Two centuries later the prophecy was fulfilled. The last Seaforth became deaf as a child and never spoke again. Although all of his communications had to be in writing, he raised a regiment, was created Baron Seaforth of Kintail, became Governor of Barbadoes, and in 1808 was made Lieutenant-General. He had four sons, the first-born dying in infancy, the second at an early age, the youngest in 1813 and the third in 1814. His daughter Mary was the widow of Admiral Hood. She later married a Stewart from the Eastern Highlands and inherited Brahan. She was driving a pony trap one day when it overturned, killing her sister. In 1815 Lord

Seaforth himself died, the last of his line.   All the remaining lands were
sold; the Isle of Lewis, Kintail, and even Brahan Castle, of which nothing
now remains. And the four lairds of Chisholm, Grant, Raasay and Gairloch
were all deformed in the ways foreseen by the Brahan Seer.

The Highland community of Glengarry here in Canada also had its
seers. Donald Joseph MacPhee, the noted violinist and music teacher of
MacPhee's Bridge near Alexandria, tells the story of one of his great-aunts
who, in the last century, reported a recurring dream in which she saw a
bòcan, a spectre, with one huge blazing eye, coming through the woods at
the north end of their farm. Many years later the first railway was put
through at that exact spot.

There are many stories of strange things that happened in the old days
in Glengarry, such as the story of *Alasdair Mór na Bóchdan,* the MacDonald who was haunted by the devil in the form of a huge hound and who finally slew him in an epic fight.

If you ask anyone here today about stories of the supernatural, you will
probably be greeted with a denial that they ever happened. But as the old
Highland woman said to the folklore collector when she was asked if she
believed in the "little people" — "Of course not! But they're there just the
same."

Heritage Day

Footfalls echo in the memory — T.S. Eliot

A Highland Heritage Day was held at the Bethune-Thompson
House in Williamstown by the Glengarry Highland Society and the
Glengarry Historical Society on Saturday, August 29th, 1992.

The day began with a tour of the Bethune -Thompson House led by
Historical Society president David Anderson, who resides there with his
wife Delande and their two children Nara and Winston.

Mr. Anderson pointed out many interesting aspects of this historic
home including the original section built by Peter Ferguson, possibly the
oldest house still occupied in Ontario. The House is owned and maintained
in the name of the people of Ontario by the Ontario Heritage Foundation.
Previous owners were: Peter Ferguson, 1784; Rev. John Bethune, 1804;
David Thompson, 1815; McLennan/Robertson family, 1836; and the
Smart/Ruxton family, 1937-1977.

The workshops opened with a discussion, led by me as president of The Highland Society, on the meaning of the English word Highlander and why it can be confusing. Although the accepted term today, there is no such word in Gaelic. To one who speaks Gaelic, the descriptive word is simply *Gàidheal,* a Gael. Everyone else is a *Gall,* a foreigner or stranger, one who does not speak Gaelic, with various labels such as *Sasunnach,* a Saxon or Englishman, (also applied to Lowlanders), *Frangach,* a Frenchman, and *Lochlannach,* a Scandinavian, from which comes the clan name *MacLachlan.*

Not all Highlanders live in the mountains and not all Lowlanders live in low-lying areas, and not all members of Highland regiments are Highlanders in the Gaelic sense. For a thousand years after the first Gaels came to Scotland (which they called *Alba*), the language of most of the country was Gaelic; even today, some 90% of the place-names in all parts of Scotland are Gaelic in origin.

The Gaels were eventually limited to the west and north of Scotland, and Lallans, the Scots language derived from many of the same Germanic sources as English, gradually took over. Today, out of a total population of about 5 million, less than 100,000 Scots speak Gaelic.

David Anderson led a discussion on the North West Company and the Highland Scots who, with the French-speaking *voyageurs,* became "the Lords of the Forests and Streams" two centuries ago and built the largest and most important enterprise in British North America at that time.

It has been said that the names of the Nor'Westers read like the roll-call of the clans at Culloden and indeed many of the Scots who travelled across Canada to the Pacific in the employ of that company were descended from Jacobite families which had suffered greatly after the defeat of the clans in 1746.

Until merged with the Hudson's Bay Company in the 1820s, the Nor'Westers had established trading posts from Labrador to the Pacific, employing thousands. In the process, men like Alexander MacKenzie and Simon Fraser gave their names to great Canadian rivers. Although MacKenzie returned to Scotland, Fraser is buried in the historic cemetery of St Andrew's West in Greater Glengarry.

Much of the history of the fur trade is preserved in the Nor'Wester and Loyalist Museum in Williamstown.

The afternoon sessions began with the genealogist of the Clan Donald Association of Glengarry-Stormont, John McCulloch, explaining how to research Glengarry family trees. He distributed a folder which gave much valuable information about finding family connections in Glengarry.

Allan Gillis, an Ottawa teacher whose roots are in Judique, Cape Breton, gave an interesting and amusing talk on the similarities shared by the Highland people of Glengarry and Cape Breton. He traced many family connections between the two places, which share much the same music, language, and customs. Gaelic has been maintained a generation or so longer in Cape Breton than in Glengarry, according to Mr. Gillis, because of the island's remoteness.

The survival of Gaelic in Glengarry was made more difficult after the railroad made Ottawa and Montreal just an hour away and ended a century of isolation.

A basic Gaelic workshop was led by Anne McKenna, Gaelic language coach, director, and accompanist of the Glengarry Gaelic Choir. She explained that to learn Gaelic (or any other language), it should be learned first through the ear. Fluency is a matter of time and practice, but a few basic words and phrases can be picked up quite easily. To help the memory, she showed how written phonetics are used, but she stressed that these vocables are only an imperfect way to learn pronunciation. To get the subtleties of the way Gaelic sounds, she stressed, we must seek out a Gaelic speaker.

Anne dictated some common words and phrases in Gaelic, emphasizing that her phonetics were only guidelines, which could be changed if individuals heard the language differently and were more at home with their own particular form of phonetics. Following are some phrases, as pronounced in Glengarry Gaelic:

How are you? (singular or informal): *Ciamar a tha thu?* Phonetics: Kimmer uh ha oo? Plural or formal: *Ciamar a tha sibh?* Phonetics: Kimmer uh ha shiv?

Answer: Fine, thank you. *Tha gu math, tapadh leat.* Phonetics: Ha goo ma, tappuh let. How's yourself? *Ciamar a tha thu (sibh) fhein?* Phonetics: Kimmer uh ha oo (shiv) hane?

Do you speak Gaelic? *A bheil Gàdhlig agad?* Phonetics: Uh vail gah-lik ackut? (There are really no words for yes or no in Gaelic. The answer consists of repeating part or all of the question in the positive or negative form, so the abbreviated response to this question could be simply *tha,* (ha) affirmative, or *chan eil,* (han yail), negative. Another response could be *tha beagan,* (ha baykin), a little).

Once the key to Gaelic pronunciation is learned (and it's not as difficult as it looks), the learner will find that there are far fewer irregularities in it than in English.

First Names

The glory and the nothing of a name — Byron

Someone recently asked me why there don't seem to be any Calums in Glengarry. It's short for Malcolm, but none of the Malcolms that I know in Glengarry call themselves Calum. Malcolm Robertson of Bainsville is known as Mackie and Malcolm McRae is simply known as Mac or Scotch Mac, a nickname chosen, evidently, for its distinction in Glengarry. Malcolm Dewar, the renowned Scottish-style violinist, just calls himself Malcolm, although I once saw him at the Glengarry Highland Games sporting a T-shirt inscribed, appropriately enough, *Calum Mór* (Big Calum).

Malcolm is a Gaelic name meaning a devotee or follower of St Columba. For some strange reason, in Scotland Malcolm is usual in the Lowlands and Calum is used almost exclusively in the Highlands.

Angus, *Aonghas* in Gaelic, is a favourite Highland name, particularly among the MacDonalds. It is a pre-Christian name and we don't know for certain what it means. In Celtic mythology the name is associated with the god who came out of the hills from time to time to arouse the passions of love (to put it mildly) and encouraged dancing, fun, and debauchery. He was sort of the Celtic equivalent to the Greek god Pan, the half-goat, flute-playing deity from whom we get the word panic.

I can't believe that any of the Anguses that I know ever indulged in pagan hanky-panky. The old origins of the word have been long forgotten and it is now a fine and respectable name.

In the 18th century the name was often written *Aeneas,* but it was not connected with the legendary Greek hero. The Gaelic pronunciation of *Aonghas* (eun-eu-uss) sounds a little like Aeneas. The "g" disappears, and it is sometimes written as Innes, as in the clan name MacInnes.

A problem with names in Gaelic is that they change spelling and pronunciation according to grammatical case, whether nominative, vocative, genitive or possessive. We don't have that problem in English and it is hard to understand unless we know Gaelic.

James, for instance, is *Seumas* (shay-mus) but not if you are addressing or calling him. Then it's *Sheumais* (hay-mish) spelled Hamish in English.

Women's names in Gaelic can be equally confusing. It's difficult to believe that Sarah or Marion is *Mórag*, (more-agh, the "g" hardly sounded) or *Mór* (more). Marion can also be *Muireall* (MOOR-al), or the English name Muriel.

Some names don't even look or sound like the English versions. Winifred is *Una* (OO-na), Jean or Jane is *Sìne* (SHEE-nah), and Janet is *Seònaid* (SHAW-net).

A popular name among Highland people is Flora, immortalized by Flora MacDonald, the saviour of Bonnie Prince Charlie. That name is spelled *Flòraidh* (Flawree) or *Fionnaghal* (F-yoonughal). Mary or Molly is *Màiri* (MAH-ree) or *Moire* (Moira), unless referring to the Virgin Mary, who is always referred to as *Muire* (MOO-ruh).

Catherine is *Catriona* (Ka-TREE-ona), an exception to the rule that the first syllable is always stressed. Christina is *Cairistine* (KAH-rist-een) or *Ciorsdan* (KURSH-tin). Dorothy is *Diorbhail* (JIRrivil), Elizabeth is *Ealasaid* (YALLusatch), Helen is *Eilidh* (AIL-ee), Harriet or Henrietta is *Eiric* (ERR-eek), Julia or Juliet is *Sìlis* (SHEE-luss), Margery is *Marsaili* (MAR-sally). Margaret is *Mairead* (MY-erat).

Men's names can also be a lot of fun. Some are easy in Gaelic, such as that most popular of Glengarry names, Alexander *(Alasdair)*. Diminutives in English are Sandy and Alec (never Alex, at least in the Scottish tradition). The Glengarry chief is always known by the patronymic *Mac Mhic Alasdair* (Mac vic Alister), the son of the son of Alexander. The MacAlisters of Loup are one of the senior branches of the MacDonells of Glengarry .

Another popular name among Highlanders is Archibald, *Gilleasbuig* (GILL-yespick), "the servant or follower of the bishop or high-priest." The "arch" of Archibald in English means "high" and "bald" refers to the tonsure, the way the head was shaved to denote the priesthood.

Here in Glengarry, Bishop Alexander Macdonell of St Raphael's was known as "the Big Bishop," *Easbuig Mór* (Esbig More) in Gaelic. The term referred not only to his position but to his prestige in the community. He was also taller than most men of his day.

Other popular men's names among Highlanders are Alan or Allan, *Ailean* (AH-leen), Charles, *Tearlach* (tchar-loch, the "h" very soft), Christopher, *Gille-Chriosd* (gillya-hree-ust), "Christ's Servant" as in the family name Gilchrist.

Colin, a name beloved by MacDonalds and Campbells alike, is *Cailean* (callan). The patronymic of the Duke of Argyll, the chief of Clan Campbell, is *Mac Chalein Mór*, "the son of Great Colin."

Duncan is *Donnachadh* (DUNN-ahug). Donald or Daniel, *Domhnall*, is one of the most difficult for a non-Gaelic speaker; "DOHN-ull" is the closest we can get in phonetics, but you have to hear it in Gaelic to get it right. I once knew a man called Donald Daniel MacDonald. "If you have a good name" he used to say, "why not use it?"

John is *Iain* (EE-yan) or *Eoin* (YOH-an). A variation is *Seathan* (Shawn), the Scots Gaelic version of the Irish *Sean.*

Kenneth, *Coinneach* (KOYN-nyuch) is a real tongue-twister. The only letters the English name shares with the Gaelic are nn, e, and h. I don't know how the name got so messed up. And Gaelic speakers have trouble pronouncing the Anglo-Saxon "th." MacKenzie, "the son of Kenneth," is worse. There is no k or z in Gaelic. Go figure.

Native Wives

À h-uile là sona dhuibh's gun là idir dona dhuibh
— *May all your days be happy ones* - Old Gaelic wedding toast

When the white men first came to America, many chose Native wives. In Canada, the early fur traders followed the routes of the French voyageurs north and west. Most of the Nor'Westers were Gaelic speaking Highland Scots, in contrast to the non Gaelic speaking Scots who were in the employ of the much older royally chartered Hudson's Bay Co.

The Bay, "the English Company," had its head office in London and sailed into Hudson's Bay annually to collect the furs brought into their trading posts by the Natives. Many of these posts were manned by Orkneymen, hired when the ships took on supplies in the Orkney Islands of Scotland on their way to America. These men were a tough and hardy breed who were often left in isolation for much of the year.

It was a little different with the men of the North West Company, which became the largest commercial enterprise in America two centuries ago. For a period of about forty years until amalgamated with The Bay in 1821, the Nor'Westers had their headquarters in Montreal and were known as "the Canadian Company." They left Montreal each season in their large cargo canoes manned by *voyageurs* and Scots, often with Mohawk paddlers from Kahnewake and St Regis. They set up dozens of trading posts as far as the Pacific.

On one wall of the Nor'Westers and Loyalist Museum in Williamstown, Glengarry, is a huge map showing the extent of these trading posts,
from Northern Quebec to what are now British Columbia and several western American states. It has been said that the names of the partners of the
North West Company read like the roll-call of the clans at Culloden.

The Nor'Westers and those affiliated with them were explorers as well
as traders. Alexander Mackenzie was the first man to cross Canada from
sea to sea, years before the Americans Lewis and Clarke did the same thing
in the United States. Simon Fraser braved the perilous river which bears his
name. David Thompson, born in England of Welsh parents and one of the
few non-Highlanders in the North West Company, was "one of the greatest
land geographers who ever lived." (J.B.Tyrell).

To become a full partner in the North West Co. a clerk usually had to
spend at least three winters in one or more of the far-flung trading posts of
the Company. Some stayed away for 20 years before seeing Montreal
again. Under such remote and lonely conditions it was small wonder that
marriages *à la facon du pays*, without benefit of clergy, were arranged. In
any case, there were no clergy there until much later.

Some men left their native wives when they returned to Montreal.
Some native wives refused to leave, preferring to stay with their own people and fearing that they would never be happy in the white man's world.
But some marriages between Nor'Westers and native women were examples of true love, faithfulness, and devotion.

The Bethune - Thompson House in Williamstown, Ontario, is named
for the noted Presbyterian minister John Bethune, who moved there with
his family in 1804 and for David Thompson who lived there from 1815.
The house is now the property of The Ontario Heritage Foundation and David Anderson, the curator, has set up a display illustrating some of the
touching stories of native wives brought to Glengarry by their Nor'Wester
husbands. Most of the following information is taken from that exhibit.

Here is a description of David Thompson's wife Charlotte Small, the
daughter of a Plains Cree and a Scots Nor'Wester, who married Thompson
in Saskatchewan, bore five children in the foothills and prairies, and had
five more children when she came with her husband to Williamstown:

> Slightly built, active and wiry. Dark skin, almost copper coloured.
> She was an excellent housekeeper and loved her home. Her only
> companions were her husband and family, very reserved in her
> ways and manner. He [David Thompson] cared nothing for society
> and showed a preference for the companionship of his wife rather
> than anyone else. (W.D. Scott, grandson).

She died within three months of David Thompson's death and they are buried together in Mount Royal cemetery in Montreal.

Nancy Small McDonald was Charlotte Thompson's sister. She became the "Indian wife" of John McDonald of Garth, who took his distinction from the place called Garth in the Perthshire Highlands of Scotland. When he retired from the North West Company he brought his wife and family to live at Inverarden, his manor house near Cornwall. He was described as gregarious, pugnacious and adventurous. For eight years they raised their family there. Then McDonald married Emily, daughter of Duncan McGillis of Rigaud and niece of Hugh McGillis, and moved into a smaller house on the estate. Nancy remained matron of Inverarden with the family of her son-in-law John Duncan Campbell, another Nor'Wester.

Glengarry residents Grant Campbell, Q.C. and his brother Atholl Breadalbane Campbell are descendants of Nancy Small and John McDonald of Garth.

Big Finnan The Buffalo McDonald brought his wife Peggy, of the Pend d'Oreille tribe of Flathead Indians in Montana, to the house which still stands on the Gore Road near Williamstown. She lived 14 years there, dying at the age of 43 in 1841. She is buried beside Finnan in St Raphael's cemetery. She was described in a letter by John A. Chisholm as "a dear little woman, who never really did catch on to what farming and all the oddities of white culture were all about."

Ann McLeod MacKenzie was the Métis daughter of Alexander McLeod of the North West Company and was raised in Williamstown with the Rev. John Bethune's family. She married local landowner "Squire" Alexander MacKenzie but died in childbirth in 1824 and is buried near her husband and son at St Andrew's Church in Williamstown. Another son, Alexander McLeod MacKenzie, became deputy-registrar of deeds for Glengarry.

Mrs. Hugh McGillis was the Indian wife of the second "Laird" of Williamstown and bore seven children in the west, all of whom predeceased them and none of whom had issue. She was sent back to the Indian country upon McGillis's return to Williamstown in 1816. He spent the remaining 32 years of his life without remarrying. The Laird's fortune passed down through John, son of his brother Duncan. There are no descendants of Hugh McGillis.

John McGillivray (Dalcrombie) of the North West Company had three sons and one daughter by a Cree woman of the Lower Churchill. In 1818, McGillivray settled on the Raisin River at McGillivray's Bridge, and married Isabella, the daughter of the Hon. Neil McLean of Cornwall. One winter, during a fierce storm, the Cree wife turned up at the McGillivray house to leave the children there for their education and care. Mrs. McGillivray received them with open arms.

Not all the children resulting from marriages *à la façon du nord* were recognized by their fathers, but many were. Catherine McDonald Grant was the daughter of Big John McDonald *le borgne* (one-eyed) of the XY Company by his Métis wife, Marie Poitras. He was the elder brother of Finnan the Buffalo. Marie was raised by her uncle, Colonel Big Jim McDonald in Gleninore (Glen Road) near Williamstown and later moved to Midland Ont. where she inherited her father's land holdings. She married Angus Grant there and there are still descendants in the Midland area.

Sainᴛ Raphael's Ruins

Majestic though in ruin — Milton

In ᴛhe Old ᴛesᴛamenᴛ the Angel Raphael was sent by God to lead Tobias through the desert and to watch over him on his perilous journey. The Knoydart pioneers who left Scotland on the ship MacDonald in 1786 chose St Raphael as their patron and after their safe arrival in the New World decided to name their church after him. With them was their priest, Alexander McDonell (Scotus), who founded the parish and built their first church, known as the Blue Chapel.

He died seventeen years later and the next Alexander Macdonell (as he spelled his name) arrived the following year. He became known as *Maighstir Alasdair Mór,* Big Father Alexander, for both his stature and his prestige. Later, after achieving great renown and being appointed to the hierarchy of the church, his Gaelic-speaking parishioners referred to him as *Easbuig Mór,* The Big Bishop.

Fifteen years after arriving in the wilds of Glengarry, he inspired the building of the new St Raphael's, which could hold over a thousand worshipers without a single pillar to block the view of the altar. This magnificent church stood for a century and a half until the interior was gutted by fire.

The roofless but still impressive ruins are maintained by an energetic non-denominational group, The Friends of the Ruins Inc. A modern chapel incorporating part of the original church now serves the St Raphael's congregation.

The name Alexander (*Alasdair* in Gaelic) is a favourite first name among Clan Donald of Glengarry, whose chiefs are always titled *Mac Mhic Alasdair* (the son of the son of Alexander). The designation Scotus, always attached to the first Fr. Alexander's name, identified him as belonging to the House of Scotus (variously spelled as Scottas or Scothouse), a cadet branch of the MacDonells of Glengarry, who were closely connected to the chiefship of that clan and could trace their lineage back to the 12th century.

The lands of Scotus (from *sgot*, a settlement) are in Knoydart, which to this day remains one of the most inaccessible areas of the Western Highlands. In this remote area the MacDonells of Scotus and their clansmen lived virtually undisturbed for centuries. The tacksmen, the "gentlemen of the clan," traditionally sent their sons to the Continent for their higher education. Thus Alexander McDonell (Scotus) was sent to the Continent to further his studies.

After several years he returned home as priest of Knoydart to find that most of the people in his parish were preparing to leave for Canada. They had many reasons for leaving but many probably felt that they could not remain in a land that no longer seemed to want them. When they finally decided to leave, their priest went with them.

This first Father Alexander was the half-brother of the legendary Spanish John McDonell who settled with his family in Glengarry around the same time.

Fifty years earlier Alexander's brother Donald, the eldest son, was in line to inherit the lands of Scotus when disaster, in the form of Bonnie Prince Charlie, arrived in Scotland. Donald, like most of his people, joined the Jacobite Rising of 1745, but he had a very serious problem. Some time before, he had arranged a commission in the British Army for his son Ranald in Campbell of Loudon's Regiment. Donald himself became a captain in the Prince's army, which, in one of the early battles of "the '45" was ordered to attack Loudon's Regiment.

The day before engaging the enemy he told the Chevalier de Johnstone, a Lowland Scot in the French service: "Perhaps tomorrow I shall have the grief to kill my own son. In going with the detachment I may be able to save his life, or stop another from killing him." Happily, Donald returned from the foray with his son as prisoner.

Several months later at the Battle of Culloden, Donald himself was mortally wounded. As he was being carried from the field by two of his men, he saw that the enemy was catching up with them. "Leave me and save yourselves," he said, "but place me with my face to the foe." The British Dragoons killed him. His half-brother chose the path of peace that ended at St.Raphael's.

The Morrisons

And we in dreams / Behold the Hebrides
The Canadian Boat Song

ORIGINALLY *O'Muirgheasain,* the Morrisons were an ancient family allied with the MacDonald Lords of the Isles. One branch of the family held the hereditary office of brieve, or judge, and were the interpreters of the Brehon laws, the old Celtic legal code.

Another branch were bards to the MacLeods of Dunvegan. There were Morrisons throughout the Highlands, particularly in the Outer Hebrides from Barra to Lewis.

Many Morrisons came to Canada with the first settlers from the Scottish Highlands. Some settled in the Greater Glengarry area. Some settled in other places across Canada, but a century ago the best known Morrison in the country was from Quebec. He was Donald Morrison, The Megantic Outlaw.

Donald Morrison's people had come to the Lake Megantic area of the Eastern Townships, a rocky and mountainous section of Quebec east of the city of Sherbrooke and north of the State of Maine. Mostly from the Isle of Lewis, these early Gaelic-speaking Scots had been so ill-treated by their landlords that only by leaving their native land could they hope to survive.

They first started coming to the Eastern Townships in 1828, about fifty years after their kinsmen had begun settling in Glengarry. Cheated out of their meagre holdings in the Highlands, they were cheated again by greedy landowners in Canada. A corporation owned vast tracts of useless land in the Lake Megantic area as well as much of the town of Sherbrooke. Gaelic-speaking agents were planted by the company aboard some emigrant ships and, during the many weeks that it took to cross the Atlantic, were often able to talk the trusting Highlanders into giving up their hopes of land grants farther west and signing up instead for miserable acres of stone and forest near Lake Megantic.

Even after generations of back-breaking labour these farms never produced more than a bare subsistence, so young Donald Morrison, as had so many before him, left for the west to earn a living. He became a cowboy and for seven years drove herds all over the west, from Alberta to Texas. Those were the rough and often lawless days of the American frontier and Donald, of necessity, became a crack shot with a pistol.

When his family got into financial trouble on the farm back in Megantic, Donald Morrison came home to help. He found that his father had been bilked by a fellow-Scot and money-lender called MacAuley. The farm was lost and Donald's aged parents were forced to live in a miserable hut, without a penny to their name.

Donald tried every legal means to get justice for his family, but to no avail. Finally, because he was not afraid to voice his opinions about the legal system and the people who had used it to ruin his family, he was accused of crimes for which he claimed he was not guilty. An American bounty hunter, with a warrant for Donald's arrest in his pocket, vowed in public that he would get him "dead or alive." When he drew a gun on him in the town of Megantic, Donald fired first and killed him.

Instead of fleeing to the States and freedom, Donald stayed for over eight months in the Megantic area, frustrating all attempts to capture him and being passed from farm to farm by loyal supporters. In spite of the offer of a large reward, no one, Scot, French, or Irish, would betray him.

Finally, under a flag of truce, he was shot by police and eventually sentenced to 18 years hard labour. He died in Montreal's Royal Victoria Hospital four years later. A short time before he died, he received a full pardon.

In 1993 we met one of the new owners of the Priest's Mill Restaurant here in Alexandria, Robert Morrison. He is descended from the rugged people of Megantic. "I'm the first generation that has no Gaelic" he sadly told us. We asked him if he was related to a wonderful old woman from Megantic whom we had met years before, Maryann Morrison. "She was my grandmother" he said, and his eyes moistened. "She died two years ago. She was a hundred and six."

I have often said in these columns that the Gaelic world is a small world. Coincidences like this seem to happen all the time, and this was one of them.

About twenty years ago an old friend, Fred MacAuley, the Gaelic Producer for BBC Radio in Scotland, wrote to say that he was coming to Canada and asked us to get some Gaelic-speakers together in Montreal to be interviewed by him for the BBC. That part was easy, but the second part of his request was a little more difficult: They had to be natives of the Province of Quebec. We called our friend Lloyd Leland, a Canadian who had learned Gaelic to be able to speak to his Lewis-born wife in her mother tongue. "That's no problem" he said. "There are lots of Gaelic-speakers from the Megantic area living in Montreal. I'll get a bunch of them together and we'll meet at your house when Fred MacAuley arrives." And that's what happened.

The star of the show turned out to be Maryann Morrison. She had come from Harris, the southern part of Lewis, on a sailing ship as a young girl. She came with her family to join relatives that had settled in the Megantic area years before: MacLeods, MacKenzies, MacDonalds, Grahams, and Macraes. She told of the hardships they had left in Scotland, of the *taigh dubh* (tye doo), the "black house" that she had been born in, the ceiling and walls black from the smoke that eddied about from the peat fire in the middle of the dirt floor, with just a hole in the roof for a chimney. But it was a good house, she said, with the cattle at one end and the people at the other. They had two beds, one for her parents and one for her and her sister. They had a table and a few chairs, a spinning wheel and a loom.

Since they had no hope of ever improving their lot, they decided to emigrate to Canada.

To get the passage money they knitted socks which they sent to be sold in Glasgow. When they had enough for the fare, they left their Island home for ever. But their trials were only beginning. For people who had never been to sea, the voyage of seven weeks was one long nightmare. They had to supply their own food, and much of it soon spoiled.

When they arrived in Montreal, they still had to make the long trip to Sherbrooke, which took a month by wagon. Then they discovered that the land they were to settle on was solid forest; the Hebrides were treeless, and they had to learn how to use an axe and saw. But Maryann Morrison never lost her faith in the future, and, with the courage and quiet dignity of her race, faced all obstacles and lived a long and honourable life. She was a very special lady. We will never forget her.

The Kilt is my Delight

Wool from the mountains, dyes from the vale, / Loom in the clachan*,
peat-fires bright, / To every strand of it some old tale—
/ Oh the tartan kilt is my delight.
Went to its spinning brave songs of Lorn,** / Its hues from the berry and
herb were spilt; / Lilts of the forest and glee of the morn / Are in his
walking who wears the kilt. — Neil Munro.
*village ** ancient area of the Western Highlands, home of the
Campbells, MacDougalls & Macintyres.

The kilt as we know it today dates back to the 18th century. It is
called the little kilt, *féileadh-beag* (feel-ya bake). Before Culloden in 1746,
the *féileadh-bhreacain* (feel-ya vre-chin), kilt and plaid in one piece, was
worn. (Plaid is pronounced as it is written, never "plad"). To don it, the
wearer would lay it out on the ground, crimp by hand the pleats that were to
go behind, lie down, and roll up in it. Here is how Edward Dwelly in his
Gaelic dictionary defines the kilted plaid:

> This consisted of twelve yards or more of narrow tartan, which was
> wrapped around the middle and hung down to the knees. It was
> most frequently fastened around the middle with a belt....The
> breacan, or plaid part...was wrapped around the shoulders, or
> fastened on the left shoulder with a brooch of gold, silver, or steel,
> according to the wealth of the wearer. By this arrangement there
> was nothing to impede the free use of the sword-arm.

After the Disarming Act of 1746, the wearing of Highland dress was
outlawed by the British Parliament. The law was ignored from time to time
by those in remote areas, but the penalties were severe enough to intimidate
most. Anyone caught wearing any form of Highland dress or tartan could
be "imprisoned or transported to any of His Majesty's plantations beyond
the seas." Many never returned from such exile. The families thus deprived
of a breadwinner could suffer extreme hardships. Any suspected of
Jacobite sympathies were required to take an oath:

I do swear, and as I shall have to answer to God at the great day of judgement, I have not nor shall have in my possession, any gun, sword, pistol or arm whatever, and never use any tartan, plaid, or any part of the Highland garb, and if I do so, may I be cursed in my undertakings, family, and property — may I never see my wife and children, father, mother, and relations — may I be killed in battle as a coward, and lie without Christian burial in a strange land, far from the graves of my forefathers and kindred — may all this come across me if I break my oath.

When Highlanders were eventually permitted to form their own regiments in the British Army, which they had not been deemed trustworthy to do for years after Culloden, the penalties of the oath were changed to enforced military service in Britain's American colonies. (Pre-1745 regiments such as the Black Watch, which was first raised in 1725, were not originally regular regiments of the line but anti-Jacobite police forces formed to keep peace in the Highlands).

The ban against Highland dress, except for soldiers, was in force from 1746 to 1782, when the Duke of Montrose succeeded in having it repealed. The only dissenting voice was that of one Sir Philip Jennings Clerke, who wanted Highland dress confined to Scotland. He had been told by an English innkeeper that when some Highland officers had stayed at his inn, the sight of the kilts and the bare legs of the soldiers had so entranced his wife and daughters that he had had to spend all his time keeping watch on them!

The only kilts seen in the early days in Glengarry would have been worn by some of the regular soldiers. Most of the fencibles (from "defensibles", temporary regiments for emergencies) wore breeches or trousers. But with the fame of Highland regiments at Waterloo and around the world and the romantic novels of Sir Walter Scott, tartans and kilts, once exclusively Highland, became the rage.

Queen Victoria, in the 1850s, furnished her Scottish residence, Balmoral Castle, with tartan from top to bottom: Tartan carpeting, tartan curtains, tartan upholstery, tartan wallpaper. The Tartan Terror had been loosed on the land, and has flourished ever since. But in this newly-discovered popularity for kilts and tartans, many strange notions evolved. Some of them will be discussed in the next column, *Tartan — Myth and Reality.*

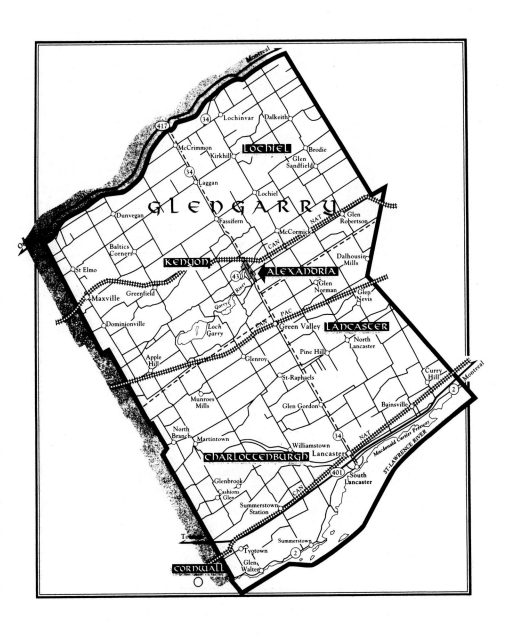

Fasg na Coille "Near the Woods" (McCormick Homestead)*Stewart McCormick.*

Frog Hollow Road, Glen Roy. *Stewart McCormick.*

" Bull-Frog Tavern " S. M. C.

Bull-Frog Tavern. *Stewart McCormick**
*Pencil sketches by Stewart McCormick (d. 1992), mostly done between
1930-1950, are courtesy of The Glengarry Historical Society
and the McCormick family.

Old Leanach Cottage, Culloden.
[Photo by Ken and Anne McKenna]

Ruined croft houses, South Uist.
[Postcard, Ken and Anne McKenna]

Big Rory McLennan. *From a portrait by
lateral descendant Deborah Kerr (1998)*

Eilean Donan Castle, Kintail. [Photo by Anne and Kenneth McKenna]

Dunvegan Castle, Isle of Skye. [Photo by Anne and Kenneth McKenna]

Sailing from Eriskay to South Uist, 1954.
[Photo Anne and Ken McKenna]

Castlebay, Barra.
[Photo Anne and Ken McKenna]

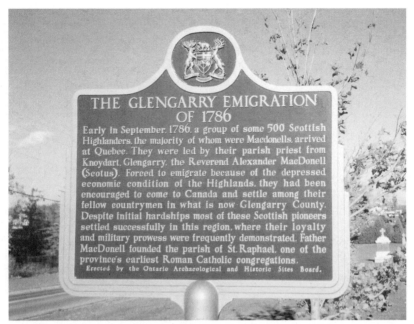

Plaque, St Raphael's churchyard, re. The Glengarry Emigration of 1786.
[Photo Anne and Ken McKenna]

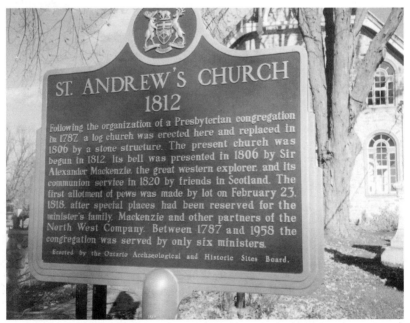

Historic plaque — St Andrew's United Church, Williamstown,
Glengarry, Ontario. [Photo Anne and Ken McKenna]

Interior, south end, Ferguson House, incorporated into
Bethune-Thompson House, c. 1780. [Photo Anne and Ken McKenna]

Interior, St Raphael's Ruins. Built c. 1820 by Alexander Macdonell, "The Big
Bishop". Gutted by fire in 1971. The church could hold 1,000 people,
with no pillars obscuring the view of the altar.
[Photo by Anne and Ken McKenna]

Fireplace and portrait of Rev. John
Bethune, Bethune-Thompson House,
Williamstown, Glengarry, Ontario.
[Photo by Anne and Ken McKenna]

Central section, Bethune-Thompson House, Williamstown; Ferguson wing
on right. [Photo by Anne and Ken McKenna]

Spinning bee on stage at Alexander Hall, Alexandria, Ont. 1913.
Notes on back of photograph state "all ladies on stage spoke Gaelic."
[Photo courtesy of the Glengarry Pioneer Museum, Dunvegan, Ontario]

Norman Stewart's Smithy, Maxville, Ont., early 1900s.
[Photo courtesy of the Glengarry Pioneer Museum, Dunvegan, Ontario]

Alexander John "Big Alex" MacIsaac
MacDonald (1865-1951), noted
Glengarry athlete.
[Photo courtesy of the Glengarry
Pioneer Museum, Duvegan, Ontario]

Capt. D. McDiarmid, Lieut. D. J. McCuaig, Major J. J. McCuaig,
Dunvegan Volunteer Infantry Coy. (No. 7, 59th Batt.)
on active service during Fenian Raids 1870.
[Photo courtesy of the Glengarry Pioneer Museum,
Dunvegan, Ontario]

A typical Glengarry scene. Beaver View Farm, Summerstown, has been in the
same family since 1784. The present owners, Archibald MacDonell and
his wife Isabel (McDonald), United Empire Loyalists,
are descended on both sides from Highland ancestors who came from
the Mohawk Valley of New York and from Knoydart.
[Photo courtesy of Archibald and Isabel MacDonell]

Typical Glengarry farmhouse.
[Photo by Ken and Anne McKenna]

Glengarry loggers in the 1890s.

[Photo courtesy of the Glengarry Pioneer Museum, Dunvegan, Ontario]

Glengarry loggers in the 1890s.
[Photo courtesy of the Glengarry Pioneer Museum, Dunvegan, Ontario.]

Glengarry loggers in the 1890s.
[Photo courtesy Glengarry Pioneer Museum, Dunvegan, Ontario.]

Fulling Bee (1926) at the farm of Duncan Donald MacSweyn, Lot 9, 9th of Kenyon, Glengarry.

[photo courtesy of Sarah MacMillan]

Dan McKercher's Sawmill, Dunvegan, Ont. C. 1890.
[Photo courtesy Glengarry Pioneer Museum, Dunvegan, Ontario]

Tartan – Myth and Reality

They were recognized among the Irish...for their exterior dress was mottled cloaks of many colours — O'Clery, 1594, describing Scots Gaels

Let's clear up a few misconceptions about Highland dress. First, a man wears a kilt, not kilts. Secondly, a plaid, pronounced as written, not "plad," is a blanket-like covering worn over the left shoulder (unless the wearer is left-handed and the plaid would interfere with his sword-arm). Tartan is the colourful material itself, but the word plaid, pronounced "plad" meaning tartan, has become so widespread that it now seems unstoppable.

There is much disagreement as to the origin of the word tartan. The Gaels remain aloof from the controversy, as in so many other things affecting the non-Gael. The Gaelic word is *breacan* (brek-in).

But what about clan tartans, as opposed to just simply tartans? How long have clans been identified with their own particular tartans? It is certainly true that multi-coloured cloth was favoured by the Gaels of Scotland from the earliest times. The Celts loved colour and ornamentation, and their choice of tartan-like material would have had more to do with taste than clan distinction. People in certain areas may have had a liking for a particular design based on availability and the local weaver's choice, so early tartans often became associated with districts rather than clans.

If a clan chief preferred a certain design, his clansmen may have followed suit, but there is no evidence that distinctive clan tartans existed before the mid-18th century. There are paintings of clan chiefs in Highland dress before that time, but the tartans they are wearing are not of any recognized clan sett or design. The "government tartan" as worn by the Black Watch and the Argyll and Sutherland Highlanders seems to be a variation of a Campbell and a Mackay tartan, chosen more for the fact that it did not show dirt and stains as much as more colourful designs, and went well with the red tunics of the day.

Two hundred years ago there were only a few tartans that could be connected with particular clans. After Culloden, tartan was outlawed except in the army, and many designs may have been lost or forgotten. Then, with the repeal of the law against Highland dress 40 years later, things began to change.

The revival of tartans and Highland dress was almost entirely due to one man, Sir Walter Scott, The Wizard of the North. In his best-selling novels he portrayed the Highlander as a romantic figure out of the misty past. Almost overnight, those who had feared and even despised the Highlander became entranced with tartans and everything that was associated with them. Much of what was believed was not necessarily true from an historic point of view, but with the exploits of Highland regiments fresh in the public mind, tartan became hugely fashionable even for Lowland Scots, who had often been the greatest enemies of everything Highland. The Noble Savage was vindicated.

Thus began the craze for "clan" tartans. Every Scot seemed to want his or her own tartan. Hundreds of different tartans came rolling off the mills, each purporting to be a genuine clan tartan. The Lord Lyon King of Arms, Scotland's supreme authority on heraldry, got into the act and all clan tartans now have to be authenticated by his office.

All kinds of rules and regulations were invented: Only those with the surname of a clan or a sept of that clan is "entitled" to wear that particular tartan, and having a mother or grandmother of the name doesn't count. But apart from "entitlement" anyone can in reality wear any tartan. All that really matters is that Highland dress be worn with good taste and with a certain respect for its symbolism as Scotland's national dress.

The Glenelg Pageant

A Report on Feis-Glengarry '94

The week of Aug. 22 to 27 was a busy one. Five days of Stanley Fraser's Summer School at Laggan, sponsored by Morlin Campbell's Glenelg Bicentennial Committee, followed by a Grand Ceilidh, supper and dance on Friday evening at the Bonnie Glen, jointly sponsored by that committee and the Highland Society, and on Saturday, *Feis-Glengarry*, the Scottish Gaelic Festival at Laggan School.

The *Feis* began at 10 a.m., with those who were prepared to sing a Gaelic song, not for marks or for competition, but purely for the joy of it. Experts in language and music were there to make positive and constructive suggestions. Everyone was encouraged. At noon there was a lunch available, organized by the Glengarry Club of Ottawa.

The afternoon featured three workshops. At 1 p.m., Michael MacConaill (the Irish Gaelic spelling of MacDonald) led a session on "The Link Between Irish and Scottish Gaelic." At 2 p.m., the Gaelic Choir and soloists demonstrated Gaelic work-songs, including a Fulling Bee. At 3 p.m., Dr. Charles Dunn of Harvard's Department of Celtic Languages and Literature and author of *Highland Settler* and *Glengarry's Gaelic Heritage*, discussed "Preserving the Highland Story." To conclude the week's activities *The Glenelg Pageant* was staged.

The pageant was written and directed by yours truly, with the collaboration of my wife Anne, the Gaelic Choir, the children of the Laggan School Gaelic Choir and Archie "Banker" MacDonald, a native of the Isle of Skye. Lighting was expertly handled by Bob Hardy, sound by Dave McCormick and Darrel MacLeod, and video taping by Michael Sandy McKenna and Bernie MacCulloch.

The Glenelg Pageant presented the story of the settlers of 1794. Although based on that particular event, most immigrations before and for many years after that date were similar: The people in a Highland district would decide that conditions had become intolerable for them. The old way of life was no more. The hereditary chiefs had become, of necessity, avaricious landlords, increasing rents that could not be paid and squeezing every penny possible out of their clanspeople. Sheep had become more valuable than people.

Most of those forced out went to the towns and factories of the south, far from their ancestral glens. They often lived in atrocious conditions, where their language, music, and culture were soon forgotten. The luckier ones raised passage money by selling all they had and joining with their families and neighbours to charter ships to take them across the ocean.

Often entire glens such as Glen Garry (which encompassed an area of about 300 sq. miles), Glenelg, Glenroy, and Glenarkaig were eventually completely emptied of their people and the few who now live there are mostly descended from those who moved in after the original inhabitants had left.

In Glen Garry, where once thousands lived, there are less than 100 today. Only one family claims to have any connection with those who lived there two centuries ago. In Glenelg, the subject of our pageant, I have never met anyone who had any connection with, knowledge of, or interest in the people who were forced out. And yes, they were forced, contrary to re-writers of history who claim that they had a choice. They may not have been bound hand and foot and carried aboard the emigrant ships while their homes were burned, as happened in the 19th century during the Clearances, but they were compelled to leave nonetheless.

When your whole way of life has been changed by outside forces that you do not understand, when the social structure of the ancient clan system has been destroyed, when your rents are doubled and then doubled again, and you feel ground down and hopeless, you have to get out, if only to give your children a future.

The year before the Glenelg incident, 1793, is known in Highland history as "the year of the sheep." That year, realization dawned on the Highland people. The great flocks of Cheviot sheep, previously thought too delicate to thrive in the north, began arriving in their tens of thousands with their Lowland shepherds, a saving boon to the landlords. But the people, their huts and enclosures, were in the way and had to go. The tacksmen (the local leaders) saw what the future would bring, and led the exodus.

This is what we tried to portray in the Glenelg Pageant. We did it in the "you are there" format: The Gaelic Choir sang *Cha Till MacCrumein*, MacCrimmon Will Never Return, with Gerry Tibbals as soloist, while the people carried their meagre belongings on board the emigrant ship. A reporter from today, with an interpreter, interviewed them. They answered in Gaelic, which was translated for the audience.

At sea, to the sound of crashing waves, the ship's passenger list was read, each name in Gaelic first and then in English. Too late in the season to navigate the St Lawrence, they arrived in Charlottetown, Prince Edward Island, in deplorable condition. As they staggered ashore, sick and feeble from weeks at sea, they were met by Highland people who were already established there. To the sound of lively mouth music, pipes and fiddle, they soon rallied and joined in a dance. The next year they reached Glengarry.

I will never forget how we all worked together in harmony to produce this little pageant. After it was over, I congratulated Gaelic Choir member Muriel Aiken for her realistic tears as they disembarked in Canada. "I wasn't acting," she said.

Dìleas gu Bàs

Mo Rùn gu Dileas — My Faithful Fair One — Old Gaelic song

To the Gaelic-speaking Scottish Highlanders, *dileas* (pronounced "jeelus") is a most important word. It means "faithful" but that is to over-simplify it. In Old Gaelic it has the extended meaning of loyalty, of faithfulness to family, clan (the Gaelic word for children) and later, to church and country. Sadly, these ancient virtues have somehow become less important in modern times or have become debased, excessive nationalism and intolerance towards others often taking the place of true devotion to family, faith, and country. But when the motto of the Stormont, Dundas and Glengarry Highlanders was chosen, they knew what they were talking about. *Dileas gu Bàs* means "Faithful unto Death."

During the month of May, 1995, we celebrated the 50th anniversary of the end of the Second World War in Europe. Anyone over the age of 55 to-day will have their own memories of those momentous days that now seem so long ago.

I was 13 years old in May of 1945 when we were lined up in the school-yard of St Leo's Academy in Westmount and the principal announced that the war in Europe was over. My best friend, John deLotbiniere MacDon-ald, jumped up and down and pounded me on the shoulders. "My brother is coming home" he shouted, tears of joy running down his face, "my brother is coming home!" I didn't have any brothers or sisters, but I had cousins who were in the armed forces and I rejoiced too.

It was hard for us to remember a time when there had been no war. For my friend John it was particularly poignant because his father had been spending most of his days in the Ste Anne's Veterans Hospital for many years. He had been gassed in the trenches of the First World War. But for most Canadians, the war was far away and we heard no gunfire and saw no bombs drop. We really didn't know many of the details of what actually had gone on in Europe until much later. We had no television and had to rely for pictures on the press and on heavily-censured newsreels in movie theatres.

But now we are fifty years older and for the past few days the media has been full of stories and pictures, some dating from the war years and some as fresh as today. We know more now than we ever knew in 1945. It is when we see pictures of the liberation of Holland that we realize what *Dileas gu Bàs* meant to the Stormont, Dundas and Glengarry Highlanders, and the Canadian graves are there to prove it.

About the only Allied soldiers that most Dutch people saw were Canadians, and you only have to visit Holland to find out that the Dutch will always remember and revere the Canadians who liberated them.

War is naturally abhorrent to all thinking people, but we must realize that if units like "The Glens" hadn't fought and died as they did, over three million Hollanders would have lost their lives. As it was, 20,000 had already died of starvation before the Canadians freed their country. And those Canadians were volunteers. They chose to leave their homes and families and travel thousands of miles to risk their lives in a cause that they believed was right. They were indeed "Faithful unto Death," and every year at the annual church parade of the Stormont, Dundas and Glengarry Highlanders it takes a very long time to read out the names of those who made the supreme sacrifice.

Now a new, updated history of the SD&Gs is being published, edited and with additional material by Brigadier-General William J. Patterson. *Up the Glens* traces the history of the regiment from its earliest days, through the Glengarry Fencibles and the Warrior Bishop, the Right Reverend Alexander Macdonell, first Roman Catholic Bishop of Upper Canada, and the proud story of "The Glens" up to the present day.

The Reason Why

How little do we know that which we are! How less what we may be!
— Byron

There are many questions about the Scottish Highland people before and after they came to Canada that I have tried to answer in these columns. One of the most puzzling is "how did the Highlanders so quickly change their allegiance from the Royal Stewarts to George the Third after their terrible defeat at Culloden in 1746?" After all, it was only a few years after George's son, the hated Duke of Cumberland, ordered the wounded Highlanders slaughtered on the field of Drumossie Moor that Highlanders, many of whom had fought against the British army, were filling the ranks of that same army.

The Jacobite Rising of 1745 has often been portrayed, in simplistic terms, as a fight between the English and the Scots. Rather, it was a civil war between two of the main elements in 18th century Scottish history; the Gaelic-speaking, mostly Catholic or Episcopalian Jacobite Highlanders and the Presbyterian, mostly Lowland and English-speaking Scots.

To complicate matters further, there were many Presbyterians on the Jacobite side and many Highland Scots on the government side, and the government forces were strongly reinforced by veteran English regiments. As in any civil war, brother fought brother and father fought son. The horrors of civil wars are shown to us today on TV direct from Yugoslavia and Africa. The Americans lost more men in their Civil War than in all the wars that they have fought since. And as Sheridan devastated the Southern States to punish the rebels, so Cumberland plundered and burned the Highlands after Culloden.

The scars and resentments ran deep, as they still do in the American South, but in the Highlands the attitude was not quite the same. The Highlanders were royalists to a man, a conviction that they shared with most of the inhabitants of Britain in the 18th century.

They were more prone to that belief than many of the new breed of town-dwellers and tradesmen outside the Highlands, and when it became obvious that the Stewarts would never return to the throne, the Jacobites slowly turned from dreams that would never come true to a new reality.

George III may have been more German then English, but that would have made little difference to the Highland Scots. He was the king, they were monarchists, and he heeded the advice of his counsellors and treated those who may have had Jacobite sympathies with benevolence, once the reprisals of 1746 ended.

As the only trade most Highlanders knew was soldiering and as the government's fear of the Jacobites abated, the ranks of the British army were eventually filled with thousands of Highland soldiers. A further inducement to loyalty was the Highlanders' knowledge that their families might be held responsible for their good behaviour.

Although some of the disbanded Highland soldiers settled in the Mohawk Valley at the time of the American Revolution joined the rebels, most remained loyal to the oath of allegiance to the British Crown that they had taken on enlistment.

It is difficult for us living in the 20th century to comprehend how the words "democracy" and "patriotism" have changed meaning in the last 200 years. To a Highlander of 1795, those words that we revere today were loathsome, conjuring up memories of the anti-royalist sentiments of the American colonists and the horrors of the French Revolution.

When Dr. Samuel Johnson said, "patriotism is the last refuge of a scoundrel," he was not denigrating loyalty and love of country, which "patriotism" means today. He was referring to the revolutions which turned his world upside down and to the rebels who called themselves "patriots."

When the American revolutionaries started attacking the loyalists, burning their homes and farms, dispossessing them and sometimes even killing them, the message was clear: "Betray your king or get out!"

And so the Highlanders of the Mohawk Valley and of the other large Highland settlement in the Carolinas had to pull up stakes and move once again. Their loyalty to the Stewart cause had brought ruination to their Highland glens and they had left their native land so that they could survive in the army, their wives and sometimes their children accompanying them, as was the custom in those days. Is it any wonder that Glengarry and Canada meant so much to them and still inspires so much loyalty among their descendants 200 years later? This is where they finally found peace.

Glengarry's Gaelic Place Names

Most of the early settlers 200 years ago came to Greater Glengarry from an area of the Western Highlands of Scotland bordered by Inverness on the north, the Inner Hebrides to the west, Argyll on the south and Breadalbane on the east. Almost all of that vast area is in the County of Inverness with the exception of North Argyll and of Breadalbane, which is mostly in Perthshire. Naturally, those first immigrants brought some of the names of their native places with them to their new homeland.

This article is about the Gaelic place names of Glengarry County, Ontario. I have not attempted to translate original French or English names into Gaelic, and have included only those places that once had or continue to have Gaelic names. As most of the names are now anglicized I include what I hope are the proper Gaelic spellings and pronunciation, and English translations. Every time I think that I have completed the list, another name turns up, but I believe that I have finally found most of them.

The County of Inverness is the largest county (or shire) in Britain. The City of Inverness, the county seat, is in the north-east of the county, and not closely associated with the Glengarry settlers. Because of its commanding situation on the Moray Firth at the mouth of the River Ness, Inverness was settled in pre-Christian times and was the capital of those ancient and mysterious people the Romans called Picts, long before the Gaels arrived from Ireland.

Later Scottish kings made Inverness a Royal Burgh and MacBeth knew it well, but as the Gaelic character of Scotland began its slow decline in the 12th century, Inverness Town became more and more anglicized and many of the present inhabitants trace their origins to non-Highland sources.

In the middle ages Inverness was more of a Lowland outpost than a Highland village, and the town council at one time even passed an ordinance stating that all "clannit men" (Highlanders) were to be outside the gates of the Town before nightfall. The incomers feared the Highlanders and often for good reason, much as some of the first European settlers in North America feared the Natives.

In the old days, about the only people from places like Glen Garry (as it is spelled in English in Scotland) who saw Inverness were those taken there to be imprisoned or hanged. The modern town of Inverness is a beautiful city now, ironically glorying in the title "the Capital of the Highlands" but it has little connection with Glengarry here or Glen Garry there.

The Gaelic spelling of Glengarry is *Gleanna Garadh* — pronounced something like "Glown-uh Garr-eh" by Gaelic-speakers. It means Glen of the Garry (river) and the exact translation of *garadh* is obscure. It probably comes from the Gaelic *garbh*, rough or uneven.

It is in the County of Inverness that we can trace the origins of most of our early Glengarry settlers and many of the place names here.

Alexandria, named in honour of the Big Bishop, Alexander Macdonell, was originally Priest's Mill, *Muileann an t-Sagairt*, pronounced "Moolin an t-Sag-urst," after he built a grist mill there a century and a half ago.

Fassifern, Am Fàsadh-feàrna, the place of the alders, "Fassaff-yarna," a few miles north of Alexandria, is just a crossroads here, and Fassfern, as it is spelled on the map of Scotland, is even smaller. It may be only a signpost now on the road from Fort William to Glenfinnan (St Finnan's Glen) but in 1745 it witnessed the Highland army marching past on its way to glory and destruction, led by Bonnie Prince Charlie. And Cameron of Fassifern and his chief, Cameron of Lochiel, (spelled, as a title, with the i and e reversed) will ever be remembered for their loyalty to that same lost cause.

Locheil *(Loch Iall)*, the body of water after which our township and village are named, (although usually spelled Lochiel here) probably means "the loch of the cattle."

Dornie, *Dornaidh,* "narrow channel of the sea, where it flows and ebbs, and where at full tide, a vessel can be towed to either side of the harbour" (Dwelly's Gaelic Dictionary), comes from the village in Kintail near the Macrae castle of Eilean Donan. The place called Dornie here in Glengarry no longer exists; only the Dornie Road remains.

The story of Glenelg, *Gleann - Eilg*, the place of the willows, "Glown Ellig" is discussed in a separate article in this book. Near Glenelg, (later Kirkhill), is Laggan, *Lagan,* a small hollow.

Glen Roy, *Gleann-Ruaidh,* the Red Glen, "Glown Roo-uh," was most probably named after the place of the same name in the Highlands, the home of the MacDonalds (or MacDonells) of Keppoch in Lochaber.

McCrimmon, Gaelic *MacCruimein*, was named for the famous family which taught the art of the bagpipe for centuries at their college of piping at Boreraig on the Isle of Skye. Some say Skye was named after a Celtic warrior-queen, but the Vikings, who were very active in the area a thousand years ago, called it *Skuyo*, Cloud Island, and that is probably the origin of the name.

The meaning of Boreraig is obscure. It is also the name of a McCrimmon family farm here, and Skye and the Skye road are nearby.

Dunvegan, *Dun-bheagan*, is named after the village on the Isle of Skye and means the little castle. Here in Glengarry it was also known earlier as *Baile na Bantraichean* "Balla na ban-trech-an," the *ch* soft as in *loch*, the Village of the Widows.

Gernish could be *Garbh-a-neas*, with several possible meanings, and is the name of a street in Alexandria. The name comes from either a place on the MacDonald island of South Uist (where it is spelled Gerinish) or from a long-forgotten site in the Highland Glen Garry.

We can't always be sure of the exact meaning of some place names in the Highlands because they are so old that the original meaning has become debatable. In our Canadian Glengarry, many names have been all but forgotten over the past two centuries and we aren't sure today how some of them were spelled or precisely what they meant.

Bra-na-houn *Bràigh na-Aibhne*, "Brah-na-Hawn," near Glen Roy, may mean the height of the river.

Another Gaelic phrase is associated with the Raisin River near Williamstown. Rhodes Grant in *The Story of Martintown, a Pioneer Village,* states that the area around Lot 24, Angus Grant's land on the 1st Concession, south side of the Raisin River, was known as *"Balla guachaidh"*, which he says was pronounced "Balla gooey." As it is on a bend or shoulder of the river, it is probably *Baile-gualaig,* meaning the place or farm of the shoulder, pronounced very much as he says. A favourite Gaelic slogan is *Clanna nan Gaidheal ri guaillibh a chèile* - Children (clans) of the Gael shoulder to shoulder. In Scotland, lower Loch Garry is known as Garry Gualag.

One mile west of Apple Hill was Carravonie *(Corra-Abhainneach),* the Twisty River, where the great mapmaker David Thompson had a potash factory.

There was a Knoydart, *Cnòideart,* near Dalkeith and a Little Knoydart near St Raphael's. *Cnòideart* is very difficult to render into phonetics—it sounds something like "Kron-dyarsht," and may mean hilly or mountainous, which it certainly is in Scotland. Even the anglicized spelling is often mispronounced. It's NOY-dert.

There is a Bockan Road (also called the Old Military Road), originally the Bockan Hill, *Cnoc Mòr a' Bhòcain,* from *bòcan,* a spectre or ghost, leading north from the village of Lochiel and another near Greenfield, *Achadh-uaine,* the name of an estate on Loch Garry in Scotland, although the Gaelic version seems never to have been used by the MacDonells of Greenfield here.

There are several "bockan" roads in Highland settlements in Prince Edward Island and Nova Scotia. Over the years, some of them seem to have been changed into Balkan roads.

There was also a Strathglass here, *Srath-ghlais,* the green valley, the home of the Chisholms in the Highlands, but nobody seems to know now where it was located. I think that the Chisholms west of Glen Sandfield may have called their area by that name at one time. Close by is Lorne, *Lathurna,* not named for the same district in Argyll but in honour of the Marquis of Lorne, eldest son of the Duke of Argyll, when he was governor-general of Canada. There is nothing there but a deserted schoolhouse.

Dalkeith, *Dail-ché,* was named for another governor-general of Canada, the Earl of Dalkeith, whose title comes from a place near Edinburgh in the Lowlands. The Gaelic meaning of the name is long forgotten but it could originally have meant Keith's field.

Not far from Dalkeith is the area known as Breadalbane, *Bràghad Albainn,* pro. "Bred-AL-ban," the upper part (or breast) of Scotland.

Angus MacRae in Maxville keeps the name of the old family homestead in Indian Lands on a sign on the shed behind his house — *Coille-Righ,* the king's forest or bush, pronounced "Koy-lah Ree."

David Livingstone-Lowe of Toronto, in his booklet *Some Gaelic Place names of Upper and Lower Canada* mentions Gleninore, *Gleann an Fheòir*, Hay Glen, for the lands of the Hay family on the Raisin River. He explains that the place name is a pun on the Gaelic for grass/hay, "feur" and the non-Gaelic surname Hay. The only trouble is that you would have to understand both English and Gaelic to get it!

Martintown was originally *Muileann Chaluim*, Malcolm's Mill, after Malcolm MacMartin. The shortened family surname then became the name of the town. In the same area is Glen Falloch, *Gleann Falaich*, the hidden glen. It is associated here with many generations of Murrays.

In Lancaster Township is Glen Nevis, *Gleann Nibheis*, named after the glen of the same name at the foot of Ben Nevis, near Fort William in Lochaber. There are several other Glens in the Glengarry area — Glen Walter, Glen Andrew, Glen Robertson, Glen Norman, Glen Gordon, Glen Donald and Glen Sandfield, but as far as I know they were never so-called in Gaelic.

If Greater Glengarry is considered to include areas beyond the actual limits of the present county and province but settled at the same period by Highland people, then the left bank of the Ottawa River in Quebec between St Andrew's East and Montebello might qualify. Some of the MacMillan immigrants of 1802 were settled in that area. Lochaber Bay and Lochaber Township there were named by them.

The difficulty with tracing Gaelic place-names in the New World is twofold; we often don't know how they were spelled because they were not written down until years later, and we don't always know if the name describes a place here or in Scotland, and the last persons to know the answers may be long gone.

Donald Simon Fraser of the Lochinvar Road has been a great help to me over the years in tracing the Gaelic place names of Glengarry and I have obtained much information from him. He tells me that the area around the south side of the intersection of the Vankleek Hill Road and the Boundary Road (now the 417 Highway) was known as *Gobhan Fuar*, "Gowan foo-ar," the cold blacksmith, because it was the farm of the man who, on his way to shanty (to work in a lumber camp), had to shoe his horse on the frozen river. Donald also tells me that Lochinvar post office was originally called MacNab, but was changed to Lochinvar by someone who probably liked the poem of the same name. It has no connection with the differently-spelled Scottish Lochinver, *Loch an Inbhir*, in Wester Ross.

Many thanks are due to David Anderson, past president of The Glengarry Historical Society, Bernie MacCulloch of Glen Roy, and Deborah and David Livingston-Lowe of Toronto for their help, advice and suggestions.

Glengarry District High School

Ged tha mi gun chrodh gun aighean —
Though I have not cows or heifers —
opening words of old Gaelic song on mural at Glengarry District High.

Is there another school in Canada that celebrates the heritage of the area in which it is situated with as much joy as Glengarry District High in Alexandria? Every year, in honour of the Highland people who first settled Glengarry over two-hundred years ago, the students of our local High School enjoy St Andrew's Day with poetry, singing, Highland dancing and pipe music. The students themselves plan the program, which also includes Highland Games events, such as tossing the sheaf and a tug-of-war.

In 1995 the festivities opened with the world-renowned MacCulloch Dancers, who filled the stage in the cafetorium, and put on their usual expert show. Then the children's Gaelic Choir from St Joseph's School, Alexandria, joined by Cassie Deprato and Angela Van der Byl, sang some Gaelic mouth music, followed by "Morag of Dunvegan." Then Elizabeth Fraser danced a graceful "Flora MacDonald's Fancy" and a reading of Robert Burns' poem "Ye Banks and Braes of Bonnie Doon" was given by Shannon Fournier.

Ian MacLeod and his daughter Ashley played some lively violin music. It is truly remarkable that Ashley is only 11 years old and has been playing for just a year. It looks like she will be the Natalie MacMaster of Glengarry in a few years. Her mother Karen on piano accompanied Ian while Ashley and her friend, Wendy MacLeod danced.

A beautiful rendition of *Ho ro, mo Nighean Donn Bhoideach*, "The Brown-haired Maiden" followed by that great teenage group that was such a hit at *Feis-Glengarry* last summer,   Meghan MacPherson, Lauren MacPherson, Roseann Kerr and Tarah MacPherson. They also sang, in English, the old favourite "The Bonnie Banks of Loch Lomond." The legend that attends this song is about two Highland soldiers who were captured after one of the Jacobite Risings. They were thrown into prison and sentenced to death. On the night before they were to be executed, one soldier was pardoned. The song represents the thoughts of the condemned man, who says that although his friend will return home to the Highlands by the "high road," the hanged man, as soon as he dies, will return instantly to Loch Lomond by the "low road," the way of the spirit.

Piper Ian Robertson played some beautiful airs accompanied by drummer Tina Bond. Ian is an excellent piper as was shown by his last selection, a very difficult jig. The playing of jigs is one of the true tests of a piper, and Ian passed with flying colours.

Cassie Deprato gave a solo performance of Gaelic mouth music, which was received with much enthusiasm. Cassie has been a member of The Glengarry Gaelic Choir for several years along with her mother Cathy.

The M.C. for the concert was Stephanie MacDonell and she did a great job. Teacher Ann MacPhee, in a tartan skirt, took snapshots of the proceedings, and teachers John R. MacDonald and Brian Filion were resplendent in Highland dress. Principal Ed Turpin and vice-principal John Danaher, with other members of the staff, joined in the prolonged applause for this wonderful expression of Canadian heritage.

Wouldn't the old Glengarry pioneers be pleased that the music and the old language of this area was still remembered, and remembered with such joy and integrity!

Locals appear on Scottish TV

From August, 1992

A crew from the BBC Gaelic service visited Glengarry recently to interview Gaelic speakers and musicians for a TV broadcast to be shown in Britain. It will be part of a series called *Anam nan Gaidheal* (The Soul of the Gael) and will trace the origins of the Scottish clans from Ireland in the 6th century to their eventual ascendancy in what became the Kingdom of Scotland. The dispersal of the Highlanders the world over after the defeat of Culloden in 1746 will be represented by the Glengarry segment.

At a hastily organized ceilidh, BBC producer Catriona MacDonald and her assistant Flora Thomson, who both hail from the Hebrides, spoke to dozens of local residents in Gaelic and English. Donald Joseph McPhee, Hugh Allan MacMillan, Allan MacPhail, Darrel MacLeod and Gerald Rory McGillis played Highland airs on their violins and the Gaelic Choir sang.

Among those interviewed were Archie (Banker) MacDonald of Montreal, originally from the Isle of Skye, Margaret Wardrop of Glen Norman, originally from South Uist, and her sister and brother-in-law Chrissie and Duncan MacMaster, visiting from Lochaber in Scotland. Duncan's mother was from Knoydart, a place that brings back memories here, and he was able to talk about the similarities between Glengarry and the Western Highlands. Members of the Gaelic Choir and the Highland Society were also interviewed.

When Anne and I brought the BBC crew to call on Alec MacDonald at his home on the 6th of Kenyon, we found the 88-year old most eager to talk to them, although, as he said, he had not spoken Gaelic since his brother's death some years before. His family was one of the last in Glengarry to speak Gaelic on a daily basis.

Alec spent several hours talking to Catriona and Flora. The visit concluded with all of us singing, at Alec's request, some of the Gaelic songs that he had known in his younger days.

After Catriona and Flora left, Alec said "I couldn't get much of the Gaelic of the blonde one, but I understood the little one fine." Catriona, "the blond one" is from the Isle of Lewis, the farthest north of the Hebrides. Flora, "the little one" is from the Isle of Barra, the southernmost of the Long Island chain that forms the Outer Hebrides. Barra is about 200 miles from Lewis. The Gaelic of Lewis has Norse overtones, while that of Barra is closer to the Irish of Donegal, which is much nearer.

Scots Gaelic was the mother-tongue of most of the people here in Greater Glengarry for over a century. It is one of the most ancient languages in the Western World and was spoken in earlier times throughout most of Scotland, as can be seen from the place-names there, which are about 90% Gaelic. It was gradually replaced by the Lowland Scots tongue and by English, and is now spoken by less than 100,000 people, mostly in remote areas of the Western Highlands and Islands and in Cape Breton.

The speaking of Gaelic was discouraged, both here and in Scotland, for various reasons, and for a long time children were punished for speaking it.

In Glengarry the story is told of the teacher in a local school in the early part of this century who had received a notice from the authorities reminding her that Gaelic was not to be tolerated, even in the schoolyard. In those days, most of the children brought their own lunches and the teacher lived with a nearby family.

As she left for her noontime meal, the teacher called aside the oldest student. "I am going for my dinner" she said, "and I am putting you in charge, Margaret. If any of the children speak a word of Gaelic while I'm away, even at play, you are to tell me when I get back." On her return, she asked if any of the children, (all of whom came from Gaelic-speaking homes), had spoken the forbidden tongue. "Oh no, Miss," said Margaret, "not one - except myself, when I told them not to."

There is a great revival of interest now in the learning and preservation of Gaelic, both in Scotland and abroad. A Gaelic playschool program was started a few years ago on the Isle of Skye and has now spread to hundreds of areas in Scotland, Cape Breton, and Canada, including Glengarry. Many involved in this Gaelic renaissance are not of Highland or even Scottish descent, but want to learn more about this beautiful language, part of the Canadian heritage, and do not want it to disappear forever.

Glasgow

But when I get a couple 'o drinks on a Saiturday /
Glasgow belangs tae me! — Will Fyffe

The largest city in Scotland and once "the Second City of the British Empire," Glasgow is a Lowland city and has been so for centuries. But as proof that Gaelic was once the main language of Scotland, Glasgow is a Gaelic name, *Glaschu*, as are many of the place-names around it; Govan, Ecclefechan, Auchtermuchtie, Milngavie, Pollockshaws, and so on. Actually, about 90% of the place-names in all of Scotland are of Gaelic origin, although Gaelic has not been spoken in most of them for as long as 500 years.

Glasgow means a lot to my wife Anne and myself, because both our mothers came from near there. Anne's grandfather Alexander "Sandy" Tait worked as a young man in the shipyards on the Clyde (a word also of Gaelic origin), the river that bisects Glasgow. My grandfather McGrory was a steel-puddler at the Blochairn Steel Works at Glasgow, at about the same time.

Sandy Tait came to Montreal before the First War to work at Vickers Shipyards. He brought his family out shortly after. He lived out his long life in Montreal and is buried in Mount Royal Cemetery. My grandfather McGrory died in Glasgow and is buried in Old St Peter's Graveyard there. Both Anne and myself have relatives in Scotland and a special place in our hearts for Glasgow.

Two of Glasgow's sons who have left their mark on Canada are John Alexander Macdonald, our first prime minister and James McGill, who gave his farm in Montreal for the establishing of McGill University. Macdonald, though born in Glasgow, was the son of a dispossessed Highland family from Sutherland and spoke Gaelic as his first language.

Glasgow began when St Mungo (or Kentigern, as he was also known), established a religious centre there in the 6th century. In the middle ages, the crest of the city included several ancient symbols, including two salmon holding rings in their mouths.

The salmon to the Gaels represented wisdom, and there are several legends associated with the items in the crest, the tree of wisdom with a bird on the top, and the hermit's bell suspended under it. The irreverent refer to Glasgow's symbols as "the bell that never rang, the fish that never swam, the tree that never grew, and the bird that never flew" and there, on the very top of the crest, is St Mungo himself, first bishop of Glasgow and predecessor of the man who visited Glengarry on Friday, September 23, 1994, Archbishop Thomas Winning.

At a special service at St Finnan's Cathedral in Alexander, Archbishop Winning was piped in by young Ewen MacKinnon, the son of Mary Ellen and Alan MacKinnon. Before and during the mass, violinists Donald Joseph MacPhee, Hugh Allan MacMillan, Allan MacPhail and Lorne Lawson, accompanied by organist Suzanne Labelle, filled the cathedral with Scottish airs.

The Glengarry Gaelic Choir sang sacred songs, including the Presbyterian version of The 23rd Psalm. When the Archbishop gave his homily, he said that he had last heard another of the songs we sang for him, *Talladh Chriosda*, The Christ Child's Lullaby, years before on the Isle of Eriskay.

At the reception after the service in the Bishop Macdonell Room at the cathedral, a large crowd pressed forward to be introduced to the special guest by St Finnan's pastor Angus Bernard Cameron. Several gifts were given to the affable Archbishop, including a copy of *Glengarry Life*, presented by past-president David Anderson on behalf of the Glengarry Historical Society, and a copy of Marianne McLean's *The People of Glengarry* by the president of the Highland Society.

Archbishop Winning thanked the gathering for the hospitality shown him and expressed his delight at the Gaelic music and at having been piped into and out of the church by such a fine young piper. "I don't think any of this could ever have happened in Scotland" he smilingly said.

Fr. Paul Bannon, the rector of St Michael's Cathedral in Toronto, who accompanied Archbishop Winning, was fulsome in his praise of the Glengarry welcome that they were enjoying, which, he said, was far more enthusiastic than they had expected. He was particularly taken by the Glengarry Gaelic Choir and stated that he hoped the choir would come to Toronto and sing in the cathedral there.

The following day, Saturday, the Scottish visitors were the guests of Msgr. Bernard McDougald at St Raphael's. Archbishop Winning was especially interested in anything to do with Alexander Macdonell, the "Big Bishop," about whom he knew a great deal.

Shortly after our distinguished guest returned to Scotland he was named a cardinal, so it's Cardinal Winning now.

The Archbishop's remarks about the Isle of Eriskay brought back many memories to Anne and myself. We had spent part of our honeymoon on that lovely wind-swept Hebridean island over forty years before.

There were no roads, inns or modern conveniences on the island then. On one of our walks through the hills we stopped at a lonely cottage to ask for a glass of water. The old woman who greeted us at the door insisted that we come in and have tea with her. She was naturally curious as to why two Canadians were visiting her remote island.

"Did your people come from here?" she wanted to know. Anne and I told her that both our mothers had been born far to the south in the Glasgow area. That did not seem to impress her.

"And your fathers, where were they from?" We admitted that both our fathers were born in Canada of Irish descent. "Well, well." she said, and brightened up immediately. "I'm Irish, you know!"

Anne and I looked at each other in disbelief. Had we actually come across an Irish person in this out-of-the-way place? Before we had a chance to ask how such a remarkable transplanting had happened, she continued. "Yes, yes, my people came over from Ireland with *Colum-cille*!" That name, as we well knew, is the Gaelic for St Columba of Iona. He and his followers came to Scotland from Ireland about the year 563.

Highland people are not overly-concerned with time. Being a gracious host and making her visitors feel at home were more important to the old lady in black with the shawl over her head than the realities of space and dates.

Eriskay lies just off the much larger island of South Uist north of Barra. It has never had a population of more than a few hundred and would have probably remained in obscurity forever except for two things: Bonnie Prince Charlie and The Eriskay Love Lilt. Eriskay was the first place where the unfortunate Prince landed on Scottish soil in 1745. He reputedly sprinkled some seeds of the Convolvulus (Morning Glory) on what is still known as *Traigh na Phrionnsa,* the Prince's Strand, and "The Prince's Poppies" grow there still. It is claimed that they will grow no other place. I picked some, pressed them in a book, and gave them to my friend Olga MacDonald, a Glengarrian working in Montreal, when we returned home.

Language, Music and Poetry

Alexander Carmichael

The collector of beauty

About a century ago a remarkable collection of Scottish Gaelic poems, songs, charms, and invocations was compiled by a remarkable man, Alexander Carmichael (1832-1912).

None of this extensive folklore titled *Carmina Gadelica* was composed by Carmichael himself (although he certainly was responsible for some editing) but was orally collected in the Highlands and Islands of Scotland and translated into English. The material eventually was published in six volumes.

Alexander Carmichael was a civil servant who spent most of his holidays and spare time gathering Gaelic folklore from people who had cherished it for generations.

It is easy to see that if he heard a poem from an old person who had been born around 1800 and who had learned it from a grandparent, we are easily transported back several centuries. Many of the Highland people who came to Glengarry two hundred years ago would have known similar compositions.

When we talk of Highland heritage we must continually refer to Culloden and its aftermath, because after 1746 and the repressive laws enacted to "pacify" the Highlands, the Gaelic way of life was changed utterly and an alien language and culture gradually replaced it.

The new order had its good points. The ancient blood feuds were ended and the arbitrary and often cruel powers of the chiefs abolished, and the Scottish Gael forced to face the modern world.

This new reality, however, eventually resulted in the depopulation of the glens and the dispersal of a proud and ancient race to the four points of the compass, often taking the memories and traditions of entire areas with them. As their Gaelic was gradually forgotten, so were their poems, their prayers, and their songs until only fragmented memories remained.

Many modern scholars, including renowned Scottish historian James Hunter, do not believe that the virtual destruction of the Highland lifestyle was inevitable. They question the hitherto largely accepted wisdom that economics were basically to blame for the plight of the Highlander, pointing to similar situations in Europe and in particular to the Scandinavian countries where more enlightened policies prevailed.

It is when we read works such as Carmichael's *Ortha nan Gaidheal* (The Invocations of the Gael) that we realize how rich and beautiful was the oral tradition of the Scottish Highlander. There were songs and prayers for daily activities from morn to night and from season to season, all accompanied by melodies that have largely been lost.

Some of the topics in Carmichael's first volume: Morning Prayers, Kindling the Fire, Milking, Churning, Sowing, Reaping, Herding, Spinning, Weaving, Guarding the Herds and Flocks, Fishing, Fulling the Cloth, Smooring the Fire (smothering the peat fire ashes at night so that the coals remained hot underneath, ready to start the fire again the next day) and finally, Evening Prayers, with perhaps a nod to the new moon and an invocation to God to protect the family, the house and the crops.

The early settlers here would have been familiar with much of this tradition. Some of the older people still claim that they prefer to pray in Gaelic, the language of St Columba and St Finnan.

Alexander Carmichael's notes give us insights into the nature of the Gael. In his introduction to Volume I he says:

> The people of the Outer Isles, like the people of the Highlands and Islands generally, are simple and law-abiding, common crime being rare and serious crime unknown among them. They are good to the poor, kind to the stranger, and courteous to all. During all the years that I lived and travelled among them, night and day, I never met with incivility, never with rudeness, never with vulgarity, never with aught but courtesy. I never entered a house without the inmates offering me food or apologizing for their want of it. I never was asked for charity in the West, a striking contrast to my experience [elsewhere].

Where did the calumny of the "cheap Scotchman" originate? Not with these people.

Carmichael describes storytellers in the Hebrides a century and a half ago. On one particular occasion he was accompanied by Iain F. Campbell of Islay, the aristocratic author of *Popular Tales of the West Highlands:*

> The hut of Hector Macisaac . . . stood in a peat-moss. . . . The hut was about fifteen feet long, ten feet broad, and five feet high. There was nothing in it that the vilest thief in the lowest slum would condescend to steal. . . . Hector Macisaac and his wife were the only occupants, their daughter being at service trying to prolong existence in her parents. Both had been highly endowed physically, and were still endowed mentally, though now advanced in years. The wife knew many secular runes, sacred

hymns, and fairy songs; while the husband had numerous heroic tales, poems, and ballads.

Hector Macisaac, the unlettered cottar who knew no language but his own, who came into contact with no one but those of his own class, his neighbours of the peat-bog, and who had never been out of his native island, was as polite and well-mannered and courteous as Iain Campbell, the learned barrister, the world traveller, and the honoured guest of every court in Europe. Both were at ease and at home with one another, there being neither servility on the one side nor condescension on the other.

It was similar with blind old Hector Macleod . . . and with old Roderick Macneill. . . . Each of these men repeated stories and poems, tales and ballads, that would have filled many books. Yet neither of them told more than a small part of what he knew. None of the three men knew any letters, nor any language but Gaelic, nor had ever been out of his native island. All expressed regret in well-chosen words that they had not a better place in which to receive their visitors, and all thanked them in polite terms for coming to see them and for taking an interest in their decried and derided lore.

But even in the heart of the Gaelic world, things were shifting fast. Changes in religion, the destitution after the Jacobite Risings and the subsequent evictions of the Highland Clearances, the national schools and the denigration of the Gaelic language all combined to destroy the ancient ways of the people. Carmichael notes the remarks of a woman which have echoes here in Glengarry:

A young lady said: 'When we came to Islay I was sent to the parish school to obtain a proper grounding in arithmetic. I was charmed with the schoolgirls and their Gaelic songs. But the schoolmaster . . . an alien like myself . . . denounced Gaelic speech and Gaelic songs. On getting out of school one evening the girls resumed a song they had been singing the previous evening. I joined in willingly, if timidly, my knowledge of Gaelic being small. The schoolmaster heard us, however, and called us back. He punished us till the blood trickled from our fingers, although we were big girls with the dawn of womanhood upon us.'

Carmichael records on another occasion:

I was taking down a story from a man, describing how twin giants detached a huge stone from the parent rock, and how the two carried the enormous block of many tons upon their broad shoulders to lay it over a deep gully in order that their white-maned steeds might cross. Their enemy, however, came upon them in the night-time when thus engaged, and threw a magic mist around them, lessening their strength and causing them to fall beneath their burden. In the midst of the graphic description the grandson of the narrator, himself an aspirant teacher, called out in terms of superior authority, 'Grandfather, the teacher says that you ought to be placed upon the stool* for your lying Gaelic stories.' The old man stopped and gasped in pained surprise. It required time and sympathy to soothe his feelings and to obtain the rest of the tale, which was wise, beautiful, and poetic, for the big, strong giants were Frost and Ice, and their subtle enemy was Thaw.

And again:

Having made many attempts, I at last succeeded in getting a shepherd to come to me, in order to be away from his surroundings. The man travelled fifty-one miles, eight of these being across a stormy strait of the Atlantic. We had reached the middle of the tale when the sheriff of the district came to call on me in my rooms. The reciter fled, and after going more than a mile on his way home he met a man who asked him why he looked so scared, and why without his bonnet. The shepherd discovered that he had left his bonnet, his plaid, and his staff behind him in his flight. The remaining half of that fine story, as well as much other valuable Gaelic lore, died with the shepherd in Australia.

The belief that music, dance, and mirth were the work of the devil was spread throughout many areas in the Highlands, particularly in the early 19th century, by certain hell-fire and brimstone evangelists. Carmichael again:

A famous violin player died in the island of Eigg a few years ago. He was known for his old-style playing and his old-world airs which died with him. A preacher denounced him, saying: 'Thou art down there behind the door, thou miserable man with thy grey hair, playing thine old fiddle with the cold hand without, and the devil's fire within.' His family pressed the man to burn his fiddle and never to play again. A pedlar came round and offered ten shillings for the violin. The instrument had been made by a pupil of

Stradivarius, and was famed for its tone. 'It was not at all the thing that was got for it that grieved my heart so sorely, but the parting with it! the parting with it! and I myself gave the best cow in my father's fold for it when I was young.' The voice of the old man faltered and a tear fell. He was never again seen to smile.

The Highland people who came to places like Glengarry and Cape Breton two centuries ago do not seem, for the most part, to have suffered from the repressions suffered by those left behind in Scotland. That's why folklorists now believe that some of the music and dances brought to Canada by Highland settlers, such as Cape Breton violin music and step-dancing, may be closer to the old Gaelic tradition that has been forgotten in Scotland. And that's why groups here in Glengarry like the Strathspey and Reel Society, the Gaelic Choir, and the Highland Society are so active in promoting the authentic Highland background that is part of our Canadian heritage. It belongs to everyone now.

The enthusiasm of the children in the schools of Glengarry for the Gaelic songs they sing so joyously is proof that the Highland tradition is in good hands and will continue to be a worthwhile contribution to the Canadian mosaic.

*The "stool of repentance" was set up in some churches. Anyone deemed to have sinned was called to sit upon it and be shamed in front of the congregation.

Women Poets in Gaelic

This is truth the poet sings, / That a sorrow's crown of sorrow is remembering happier things — Tennyson

On television recently there was a dramatization of a talk given some sixty years ago at Oxford by the English writer Virginia Woolf. In it she stated that there were very few English women writers or poets before the 19th century. This started me thinking of our Gaelic poets. Although the great majority were men, in keeping with the male-dominated society that existed in all areas, there were many women poets in Gaelic Scotland for hundreds of years before 1800.

As the population of Scotland was only one-tenth of the population of England and those speaking Gaelic after 1600 were a still smaller proportion of the Scottish total, the number of women poets among the Highland people was remarkable. Apart from anonymous love songs to men which we can assume were written by women, some of the greatest poems in Gaelic were composed by women.

Derrick Thomson, the modern Gaelic poet, writing in *The Companion to Gaelic Scotland* published in 1983, lists ten women poets from as early as the 16th century. Since almost all Gaelic poetry until modern times was handed down orally, only fragments have survived, a few drops of what must have been an ocean of words.

It is easy to understand the Gael's love of poetry. From pre-Christian times to the destruction of the clan system in the 18th century each great family had its own bard whose duty it was to extol the virtues and perpetuate the accomplishments of the chief and the clan, and there were many clans. Edward Dwelly in his monumental Gaelic dictionary of 1901 describes the bard and the love of poetry among the Gaels:

> Poetry being, in the opinion of the warlike Celts, the likeliest method of perpetuating their bravery, the bards were held by them in the highest veneration. Princes and warriors did not disdain to claim affinity with them. The Celts, being passionately fond of poetry, would listen to no instruction ... unless it were conveyed in rhymes. We often find a bard entrusted with the education of a prince, and about three hundred years ago, a Highland chief had seldom any other instructor.... Among the Irish Celts the bards enjoyed many extraordinary privileges. The chief bard was called *Filidh*, or *Ollamh ri dan*, a graduate or doctor in poetry, and had thirty inferior bards as attendants, whilst a bard of the second order had fifteen. The Gael of Scotland was not behind his brother Celts in his veneration for the bards, for they had land bestowed on them, which became hereditary in their families.

The English consider it sufficient to have one poet laureate at a time. In the Highlands, it was as if there were dozens of poet laureates busily turning out hundreds of poems, each trying to outdo the other and living off the fat of the land. Indeed, by the 17th century there were so many bards that they were considered a nuisance and laws were passed severely restricting them.

But apart from these professional bards there were great numbers of poets who composed without hope of recompense. Most women poets belonged to this latter group.

Gaelic poetry was always sung or chanted. Poetry and song were indivisible. In the oral tradition combining words and music helped the memory, and memory was the pride, and sometimes the curse, of the Gael.

Anna Gillis or MacGillis, 1759-1847, from Morar in Clanranald country, married a MacDonell of Knoydart. Before she left the Highlands for ever to settle in the Glengarry settlement in 1786 she composed *O, Siud an Taobh a Ghabhainn* (That is the Road I Would Take). It is always difficult to translate poetry fluently from one language to another, and it is particularly difficult when the words are composed with a melody in mind, with each syllable tailored to fit the nuances and grace notes of Gaelic music. Often the best that can be achieved is a literal or basic translation without the figurative sense that is an essential element in Gaelic poetry.

These translations of Anna Gillis' poems are from *The Emigrant Experience* by Sister Margaret MacDonell of Antigonish, Nova Scotia:

> We'll take leave of Morar, / Arisaig, and mountainous Moidart, / Eigg, and fair, surf-swept Canna / and beautiful, lovely Uist. / That is the road I would take; / that is the road I would take; / and wherever the road lay / I would take it for I know it well.

That is the first verse. The rest of the poem is taken up with yearning for a land of peace and plenty. The poem ends:

> We shall leave the land of the lairds; / we'll go to the land of contentment, / where there will be cattle in the folds / and around the fine pools.

> We shall leave and not delay; / we'll bid you all farewell. / We'll sail over the billows. / God speed us.

After coming here she wrote *Canada Ard* (Upper Canada) from which these lines are taken:

> Young Father Alexander, / son of Scotus of the banners, / the holy priest, was full of kindness. / Like a saint he brought us out / so that we would be free / as were those who followed Moses out of Egypt.

> We got farms of our own / with proprietary rights from the king, / and landlords will no more oppress us.

Father Alexander McDonell (Scotus) came with his Highland people to Canada and stayed with them to the end of his life.

Anna Gillis, in spite of her high hopes for the future, found the endless forests of Glengarry and the drudgery of clearing the land almost too much to bear. She fell into a deep depression and only rallied when the priest was able to convince her that the hard life in Canada was still better than the hopelessness of life in the Highlands.

For the Gaels, who had a mystical love of the land of their birth and the burial places of their ancestors, leaving it all for an uncertain future was hard indeed. But in Canada they found what they wanted; contentment, and their own land.

The Pipes of Glory

To the making of a piper goes seven years and seven generations
— Highland adage

Before the introduction of the violin in the 17th century, Gaelic Scotland had but two musical instruments in general use — the Celtic harp or clarsach, and the bagpipe, the "great war-pipe of the Gael."

Although most nations had some form of bagpipe from the earliest times, only the Highland pipes and the music composed for them has achieved universal renown. From an instrument played in relative obscurity by a few individuals in Scotland and Ireland in the Middle Ages, it has become the chosen instrument of thousands of devotees worldwide, many of whom have no Highland or even Scottish blood in their veins.

The chanter of the pipes, on which the melody is played, has only nine notes, and because it predates the modern musical scale has a slightly Oriental tone. That is one of the reasons why the Highland pipes have become so popular in the Middle East, India and Pakistan.

It is only within the past two centuries that pipe music has been transcribed. Before about 1800 piping was taught through *canntaireachd,* pronounced "kannter-ak" a complicated series of vocables in which each note and grace note was identified.

The Bretons of France, distant Celtic cousins of the Gaels, are very fond of piping. In recent years their particular form of bagpipe has been largely replaced by the Highland version and Breton pipers regularly compete (and win) at Scottish Highland Games.

As the Scottish writer Neil Munro wrote in *The Oldest Tune in the World :*

The Breton people canntarach too, like ourselves — soft-warbling them to fix in the memory — the same wind blows through reeds in France and Scotland, and everywhere they sing of old and simple things; you are deaf indeed if you do not understand.

Perhaps that explains the appeal of the pipes — something elemental, something that strikes a chord, a distant memory of a simpler time when we were more in tune with nature.

Neil Munro again:

The fast tune with the river in it, the fast river and the courageous, that kens not stop nor tarry, that runs around rock and over fall with good humour, yet in no mood for anything but the way before it.

Any talk of the great Highland bagpipe must include the story of the MacCrimmons of Skye, hereditary pipers to the MacLeods of Dunvegan and teachers of the art of piping for centuries at their school at Boreraig.

In *The Pipes of War* by Sir Bruce Seton and Pipe-Major John Grant, tribute is paid to this legendary family:

Today, cattle browse upon the site of the MacCrimmon College, within whose walls instruction on the piob-mhor had been given to countless students. Thither had come the best pipers of Scotland to receive the finishing touches to a piping education well-nigh perfect in itself, including representatives of the three other well-known piping families, MacArthur, Mackay and Campbell.

The MacCrimmons taught *céol mòr* (kyole more), the original form of piping, now commonly referred to as pibroch, although that word simply means piping. It consists of a theme followed by many variations, which pipers in the Highlands were playing long before that particular musical form was perfected for the organ by J. S. Bach.

Until the pipe band came into fashion in the British army in the 19th century, all piping was solo piping, the clan piper inspiring the clan regiments in time of battle or playing laments or salutes in memory of the famous.

Music was so much a part of the Gaels that the notes of the pipes often seemed to speak to them in a language that only they could understand. There is at least one tale of a piper, imprisoned in an enemy's castle, sounding a warning to his clan of an impending ambush by playing a combination of notes understood only by his own people.

The fame of the MacCrimmons gave rise to many legends. This is one of them: Over three hundred years ago, Iain Dall (blind) Mackay of Gairloch, himself a great piper, having taught his son all he knew, sent him to the MacCrimmons to perfect his playing.

When he returned home after several years of tutelage he brought with him the greatest MacCrimmon piper of the time, Patrick Og. They decided to play a trick on the old blind man. "When we near my father's home," said the young Mackay, "make no sound, and he will think me alone. After he greets me, he will ask me to play, but you play in my stead." Sure enough, that is what happened. As the great MacCrimmon played, tears rolled down the grizzled cheeks of the sightless man. When Patrick Og finished, Iain Dall shook his head in wonder. "The light may have gone from my eyes," he said, "but not the understanding from my mind. That was the playing of Patrick Og MacCrimmon, and no other."

In *The Pipes of War*, another anecdote is recorded:

> At a gathering the King was reviewing his troops. He saw about eighty pipers standing around, all bareheaded except for one old man in the middle who wore his Highland blue bonnet. The King asked who the man in the centre of the group was who seemed to be their leader. 'Sire,' he was told, 'you are our King, and that old man, Patrick MacCrimmon, is the Prince of pipers.' The King called him by name and gave him his hand to kiss. MacCrimmon, on the spot, composed the pibroch *I got a Kiss of the King's hand.* It is still played to this day.

Another of Patrick Og's greatest compositions is *The Lament for the Children,* in memory of the deaths of his eight sons from fever in a single year.

There were several other schools of piping in the Highlands. The MacIntyres were hereditary pipers to the MacDonald Lords of the Isles, the MacArthurs to the Campbells of Argyll, and the Mackays of Gairloch were second only to the MacCrimmons.

But piping schools faded out after the defeat of Culloden in 1746 and the destruction of the clan system. The Disarming Acts, imposed by a vengeful government until repealed in 1782, outlawed tartans and Highland dress. Only as soldiers in the British army could Highlanders play the pipes in their traditional garb. Ironically, the survival of piping was ensured in the Highland regiments by the same British government that had once tried to destroy so much of the Gaelic way of life.

Of course, army piping was different, adapted for marching and drill, for sounding reveille and lights out, announcing mess time and the various duties of a soldiers day, and for dancing at military balls. Pibroch was reserved for the officers' mess, but there were still some individuals in remote areas in the Highlands who struggled to keep the ancient tradition alive.

Around 1800 the MacCrimmons had a dispute with the titular chief of the MacLeods of Dunvegan, by then reduced to nothing but a landlord, and many moved to Glenelg, on the mainland opposite Skye. The traditional Highland allegiance to the clan chief was gone and the chiefs' hereditary powers were no more.

Within a few years, most of the MacCrimmons had left the Highlands. Many came to Glengarry, where there is a place called McCrimmon. One of the McCrimmon farms in the area is known as Boreraig, and a few years ago a young man from Western Canada whose roots were here in Glengarry won the top award for piping in Scotland. His name was McCrimmon.

> But while the grass grows green on the spot where the college stood, the memory of these master musicians is enshrined in the ancient traditions of the Island, in the MacCrimmon compositions preserved and played today . . . the fame of the MacCrimmons will never die as long as the memory of them remains, and the honour due to these Kings of Pipers will be enshrined in the music they left behind them. *The Pipes of War.*

One of the most touching of laments, *Cha Till MacCrumein*, MacCrimmon Will Never Return, was composed by Donald Bàn MacCrimmon before he marched off with the MacLeod chief to die in one of the early battles of the '45. He had dreamt that he would never return, and his vision came tragically true. The pibroch was made into a song, some say by his sweetheart, and is sung by the Glengarry Gaelic Choir.

Every year on Remembrance Day pipers are called on to play laments at memorial services. It is appropriate that the Highland bagpipe is featured on these occasions. No other instrument can inspire troops or arouse pathos like it.

But the men who played the legendary pipes in battle paid a terrible price. In the 1914-1918 War, over five hundred pipers were killed in action and thousands were wounded. The heroism of ancient times was no match for machine guns and high explosives.

The terrible casualties among pipers eventually caused them to be barred from leading men into battle. But it was too late for many of the greatest pipers of the day. An entire generation of pipers lies buried in the mud of France and Flanders, many of them volunteers from Canada. After the First War there were few pipers left in Glengarry.

This is a poem from that war by E.A. Macintosh, inspired by MacCrimmon's Lament:

> The pipes in the street were playing bravely /The marching lads went by /With merry hearts and voices singing /My friends marched out to die. /But I was hearing a lonely pibroch /Out of an older war / 'Farewell, farewell, farewell MacCrimmon / MacCrimmon comes no more.'

> And every lad in his heart was dreaming /Of honour and wealth to come /And honour and noble pride were calling /To the tune of the pipes and drum /But I was hearing a woman singing /On dark Dunvegan shore, / 'In battle or peace, with wealth or honour, MacCrimmon comes no more.'

> And there in front of the men were marching /With feet that made no mark /The old grey ghosts of the ancient fighters /Come back again in the dark /And in front of them all MacCrimmon piping /A weary tune and sore / 'On the gathering day, for ever and ever, /MacCrimmon comes no more.'

Mouth music

The oldest form of Gaelic song?

Mouth music is *puirt-a-beul* in Gaelic, pronounced "porsht-ah-beeul" in English phonetics. It was originally composed to be sung for dancing when a piper or fiddler was not available. Today it is sung for pure joy and is often accompanied by keyboard, percussion, or other musical instruments. It is unique to the Gaelic people of the Scottish Highlands and their descendants in places like Cape Breton and Glengarry. Unlike "diddling," as in "dee dee diddle dee dee," actual words are sung. It seems to be unknown elsewhere, even in Ireland, although in Quebec a similar form of music is sung, unheard-of in France, possibly deriving from early Gaelic-speaking settlers.

True *puirt-a-beul* has to have three essential ingredients: The cadences, intonations and grace notes of the Highland bagpipe. This does not mean that the actual sound of the pipes is imitated, but the Gaelic words are carefully chosen to represent the intricate fingering of each individual tune on the pipe chanter. This is far more complicated than merely humming nasally as is done when someone tries to make a sound like the droning of the pipes. In other words, *puirt-a-beul* represents the subtle Celtic art of blending words and music so that they become one indivisible entity.

With *puirt-a-beul* the meaning of the words is secondary to the sound; the words are real but often nonsensical. Mouth music is for dancing, and the important thing is to get feet tapping with the irresistible urge to leap up and dance the delightful reels, jigs, and stately strathspeys that distinguish Highland music.

Sadly, this inherent love of music and dancing among the Highland Scots was once severely restricted and even abolished in many areas. In the 18th and 19th centuries a strict form of fanatical religious puritanism was introduced to large parts of the Highlands which resulted in the suppression of much of the joyous music of the Gaelic people. They were told that dancing was sinful and music was the work of the devil. In certain areas this repression was so strong that bagpipes and fiddles were thrown into bonfires and no one sang again. Many never smiled again, either, and a sadness descended on the people. The cheerful, exultant Highlander was turned into the dour, stern Scot, an image that remains with us today.

Even Walt Disney in the cartoon version of Dickens' *A Christmas Carol* had to turn the nasty Englishman Ebenezer Scrooge into the mean Scot MacScrooge. Is it any wonder that the impression of the Scot as a kill-joy is so prevalent? Talk about bad press! Unfortunately, as in most generalizations, there is an element of truth in it. But there is another side to the story.

Doom and gloom may have been the order of the day in certain areas of the Highlands, but many areas were unaffected. It was mostly from these happier districts that the people came who settled in Cape Breton and Glengarry.

The famous Presbyterian minister John Bethune, who lived in Williamstown two centuries ago, was reputed to have enjoyed the music of his native Highlands and may even have played the pipes, or at least played the practice chanter. When he enjoyed a visit with his great friend Bishop Alexander Macdonell, as often happened, we may be sure that they sometimes enjoyed a Gaelic song together, and an exchange of the stories, poems and legends of their people.

Today the popularity of the Gaelic music of Ireland and Scotland is greater than it has ever been. Under the evidently more politically correct term "Celtic," a new generation of musicians is taking to the concert stage free of the guilt imposed on a joyous people a long time ago by the haters of beauty. The music of Clannad, De Danaan, Run Rig, Capercaillie, the

Barra MacNeills, the Rankins, Natalie MacMaster and Tracey Dares, Ashley MacIsaac, Phenigma and so many others (including our famous Glengarry Gaelic Choir) is the folk music of the twentieth century. Wouldn't the old nasties be surprised!

Why sing in Gaelic?

Confessions of a Gaelic singer

As a member of the Glengarry Gaelic Choir I'm sometimes asked why we sing in Gaelic. After all, hardly anyone speaks the language any more. Why don't we simply sing our songs in English so that everyone can understand?

There are several reasons why we sing in Gaelic. First, the choir is a *Gaelic* choir, not an English choir, and the words of our songs were very carefully chosen to go with the music. There are thousands of choirs and soloists the world over singing Gaelic songs in English, although they are generally unaware of it.

Many Scottish songs are derived from Gaelic compositions. We sing them in the original versions and try to give the listeners a brief synopsis of what the songs are all about.

The truth is that most songs sound better in the language in which they were composed. Every once in a while Italian, German, French or Russian operas are sung in English. It seldom seems to work. True opera lovers prefer to follow the translated libretto while the opera is sung in the language in which it was composed. It sounds better that way.

When an Italian opera is translated into English, for example, the words are often twisted out of shape to suit the music, and the special blend of language and music is lost. Most times the English words are unintelligible anyhow, so it might just as well be sung in the original.

This marriage of words and music is most important in Gaelic singing, because in the Celtic tradition the sound of the words is as important as the sound of the music.

The story is told of the folk-song collector who was trying to get the words of a traditional Gaelic song from an old man. "Just give me the words" she said, "I already know the melody." "Give you the words without the music?" he said. "That is impossible. They cannot be separated!" And that was that.

From the most ancient times, all Gaelic poems were composed to be sung. Even modern Gaelic poetry is often recited in a sort of chant, because sound is fundamental to the Gael.

Another reason why we sing in Gaelic is to honour the memory of those who came before us and whose mother tongue was Gaelic. The Glengarry Gaelic Choir sings in the old language of Glengarry. It is part of our Canadian heritage and we do not want it to disappear. It has as much right to exist as any other language. If it is no longer heard, the world will be the poorer for it, but that will never happen as long as we sing these beautiful and joyous songs and share our love of "the lion's tongue".

George S. Emmerson in his definitive 1971 book *Rantin' Pipe and Tremblin' String* suggests that the music of the Gaelic-speaking Highlanders was the source of most of the folk music of Scotland. That musical tradition came from Ireland with the Dalriadic Scots in the 5th and 6th centuries.

The music was not written down until the Middle Ages and there were no recording machines until recently, so we can only guess at how it sounded originally.

The music would have evolved, of course, over the centuries, but it would have been obviously closely related to the music of the Irish Gaels. But there are two distinct forms of that Celtic tradition that became unique to Scotland;   mouth-music, known in Gaelic as *puirt-ah-beul* (pro. porsht-u-beeul), and the strathspey. As Emmerson says:

> *Puirt-a-beul* . . . is the product of a primitive impulse to associate all music with words, or rather, with uttered syllables, whether they make sense or not. The use of meaningless syllables . . . is encountered in the music-making of primitive societies, particularly of the North American Indians. Thus *puirt-a-beul* is compatible with a very ancient origin, even pre-dating instrumental music . . . [it] usually comprises a jumble of meaningless syllables and sundry comic phrases. Although *puirt-a-beul* is used for dancing, it also finds application as work-song. In tasks requiring the co-ordination of a number of workers the work-song is of inestimable practical help. . . The *ioram* (boat song) was rarely far from the lips of oarsmen, and indeed there are songs for every task, such as spinning, herding, and milking. . . The work-song in the British Isles has survived longest in the Gaelic-speaking communities, and there is no doubt that the Celtic tradition fosters this as it does singing of all kinds at every opportunity.

Here in Glengarry many can recall their mothers or fathers singing a Gaelic song as they milked. They believed that the cow gave more milk that way and both milker and milkee were more contented.

The Cape Breton Choir Visits Glengarry

'S e Ceap Breatainn, tìr mo ghràidh / Cape Breton, land of my love
— theme song of the Cape Breton Gaelic Choir

What a joy it was to have the Cape Breton Gaelic Choir as special guests at the 1995 Highland Games! They sang at the Concert before the Games to an audience of about seven thousand, on Saturday morning and afternoon at the Clan Building on the Games grounds and at St Raphael's on Sunday morning.

The Glengarry Gaelic Choir also sang at the Friday show and twice on Saturday afternoon — once after the Cape Bretonners and again at Sine's Gaelic Language and Song workshop. What a feast of Gaelic, the old language of Glengarry! As Donald Simon Fraser, the Lochiel historian said: "I never thought I would hear our ancient language spoken and sung by so many after it almost died out." There were tears in many eyes as the sweet cadences of Gaelic song filled the air, and thousands who had never before heard it showed their approval with thunderous applause. The Glengarry ghosts must have been smiling the whole weekend long.

The Cape Breton Gaelic Choir was directed by Mae Cameron, an octogenarian whose energy and enthusiasm put many half her age to shame. The choir is the result of her dream, and her dream has certainly come true.

The forty members of the choir include men and women from all walks of life and from various religious backgrounds. There are even a few retired nuns and priests among them. It is a truly ecumenical group, much like our Glengarry Choir.

When we started our choir here in 1990, to celebrate the centenary of St Finnan's Cathedral, United Church minister Colin MacDonald agreed to become our first conductor. One of the first Gaelic songs we learned was *Crodh Chaillein*, "Colin's Cattle". A local wag, observing the religious affiliation of the choir members, dubbed us "Colin's Catholics" and that's how it was until Darrel MacLeod joined. Today the choir is representative of the entire Glengarry community.

There are other similarities: The two choirs sing many of the same songs, in slightly different versions, and Mae Cameron agrees with Anne McKenna that competitions based on rigid rules and regulations take a lot of the joy out of Gaelic singing. After all, this music was composed for enjoyment, for expressing emotions and spirituality and each Gaelic-speaking area, in Scotland or in Canada, would sing the songs in their own way.

Canadian Gaels inherit Celtic traditions going back thousands of years. One of the main characteristics of the Celts noted by Roman writers was a fierce individuality and a love of freedom. This was not exclusively a Celtic trait, of course, but the Celts seem to have raised it to an art. They didn't like large settlements, preferring to live in widely scattered communities, and although renowned for their fighting abilities, they did not take to discipline and were difficult to control for any length of time, causing their enemies to scoff at their inability to unite in a common cause.

What the Celts held as a virtue, that passion for individual freedom, became a liability when better-organized forces attacked and subdued them. That same virtue applies to their music, and any attempt to dictate how a song must be sung inevitably leads to stagnation and the loss of that intangible magic that is the characteristic of Gaelic music.

There are limits, of course, and the words and music must not be altered out of all recognition, but most folk-song exponents now believe that variations and individual interpretations of traditional songs should not only be accepted but encouraged. For centuries, outsiders have imposed rules on the culture of the Highland Scots, from how their music and dance must be performed, to how Highland dress must be worn and over which shoulder a woman should wear a tartan sash.

The old Highlanders would scoff at such "rules." Strict regimentation was foreign to them. That is why we do things our own way here in Glengarry and the Cape Bretonners do things a little differently. We are all Canadians now and our heritage owes as much to this country as to Scotland. If each glen in the old country had its own way of doing things, why should places here, a thousand miles apart, be identical?

When the Cape Breton Gaelic Choir sang during mass at St Raphael's, the 40-member choir filled the back of the chapel which is built onto the west side of the ruins. The choir sang four times during the service, filling the church with the language and music that belongs to Glengarry and which was spoken and sung by the Highland Scots who built the huge stone church there in 1821.

The portrait of the "Big Bishop," Alexander Macdonell, looked down on the scene. Some of us who were there imagined that we saw him smiling. After all, Gaelic was his mother tongue as it was for his congregation. St Raphael's must be the only place in the world outside of Cape Breton where you can see a tombstone inscribed "noted Gaelic singer."

Back in the 1930's news reached Cape Breton from Scotland that *Cille Choirill*, the ancient church of the MacDonalds of Keppoch near Glen Roy in Lochaber, was falling into ruin. There has been a place of Christian worship on that site, high on a cliff overlooking some of the most rugged scenery in the Highlands, since the 6th century.

A newer church in nearby Roy Bridge, St Margaret's, dating from 1826, had succeeded *Cille Choirill*, but most of the original population was already in Canada. Many were in Cape Breton, and some in Glengarry, but it was the people of Cape Breton and in particular those in the Mabou area who answered the call to help restore the old church. They were the descendants of those MacDonalds, MacDonells, Campbells and MacMasters, among others, who revered the memory of their "chapel on the cliff," even if most had never seen it.

They collected enough money to restore the church, and when help was needed again recently, the Cape Brothers responded as they had sixty years before, and *Cille Choirill* was saved a second time.

It was very fitting that the Cape Breton Gaelic Choir sang at St Raphael's, just when *The Friends of the Ruins* were launching their campaign to save the walls there. If a few dedicated people can generate enough enthusiasm to save the ruins of a church three thousand miles away, how can we fail to save the ruins of a place right here that is so much a part of Canada's heritage? Let's hope that the beautiful sound of the Gaelic music sung by the Cape Breton Choir at St Raphael's will echo across Canada and the U.S. and that the message of *The Friends* will be heard.

Our own Glengarry Gaelic Choir sang recently at the Macdonell - Williamson House. This imposing stone building was built by a son of "Spanish John," John le prêtre Macdonell, a partner in the North West Company, in 1817. For many years it was an important carrying-place and store for the fur traders portaging past the Chute a Blondeau (Long Sault) and for travellers passing up and down the Ottawa River.

In 1978 the Ontario Heritage Foundation acquired the house to save it from demolition, and now the *Friends of the Macdonell - Williamson House* is dedicated to the preservation, restoration and re-opening of the site. The Macdonell House is situated on the Ottawa River on the Ontario-Quebec border at Point Fortune, just off Hwy. 417.

Pride in our heritage makes us proud Canadians. As Edmund Burke said two hundred years ago: *People will not look forward to posterity, who never look backwards to their ancestors.*

The Macintyres

Gabhaidh sinn an Rathad Mór — We Will Take the Good Old Way
— Pipe tune of Clan Macintyre

On one of our first trips to Scotland some forty years ago we were told by friends in Glasgow not to miss what they referred to as "the most fashionable tweed shop in the country" in Fort William in the Highlands.

Anne and I were just beginning to learn Gaelic at the time and were not very familiar with how names were spelled in that language. When we got to Fort William, we walked up and down the High Street looking for what we had been told was Mary Macintyre's Tweed Shop. There *was* a tweed shop, right enough, with a beautiful display in the window, but the sign, in Celtic lettering, read *Mairi nic an t-saoir*. Then it dawned on us: Macintyre means Son of the carpenter, *Mac an t-saoir. Nic an t-saoir* is in the feminine, Daughter of the carpenter. Eureka! It certainly looked a lot different from the way my cousins in Glengarry, the Mcintyres, spelled their name, but we were thinking in English and looking at Gaelic, which, as any learner soon finds out, can be very frustrating.

Rather than going into all the variations of the English spellings of the name, we'll use Macintyre in this column, unless we are referring to a particular family who spell it differently.

The spelling of Gaelic names in English is always controversial, particularly when the same name may be spelled in many ways and each variation is stoutly defended as being the only correct one. Because Macintyre refers to a trade and not to a descendant of an individual, the only letter that should be capitalized is the first, as in all personal names, but that's not a big deal. Carpenters (or joiners as they are sometimes called in Scotland) are scattered throughout the land, so all Macintyres are not necessarily connected. Each clan or district would have one or more families so identified, originally only as a nickname, later as a proper or family name.

The principal clan was closely allied with Clan Donald, and would have probably called themselves MacDonald when away from home. Other Macintyres were a sept or branch of the Campbells of Creignish in Argyll, others were connected to the Stewarts of Lorn, and yet others identified with the Macintoshes. The hereditary pipers to the MacDonalds of Clanranald were Macintyres, just as the MacCrimmons were pipers to the MacLeods of Dunvegan.

The most famous person to bear the name Macintyre, at least to Gaelic speakers, was the poet Duncan Bàn, *Donnchadh Bàn*, (pronounced something like Donn-ach-ah Bahn), fair-haired Duncan. He was born in 1724 in the hills of Glenorchy, Breadalbane, Scotland and died in 1812. The first edition of his poems was published in 1768, and many of the early Highland settlers in Glengarry and other parts of Canada would have been familiar with his poetry.

Although Duncan Bàn, like most Gaelic speakers of his day, could not read or write the language and would not have cared how his name was spelled, he was heir to the ancient bardic tradition of Gaeldom which stretches back before recorded history.

His poetry covers many subjects, from songs of praise for his Campbell chief to songs describing the beauty of his native glen and the wild creatures that lived there. He was particularly fond of the red deer that abounded on the slopes of the Highland hills and his lines depicting a sleeping fawn are among the most delicate and touching in Gaelic poetry.

He made several poems in praise of Gaelic and the pipes for the Highland Society of London between 1781 and 1789. That Society was the model on which the Highland Society of Canada was based in 1818 and is now known as the Glengarry Highland Society.

Duncan Bàn's most famous work is a long narrative poem translated as *In Praise of Ben Dorain,* a mountain in Breadalbane which the poet saw every day during the many years he lived in Glenorchy.

Because Duncan Bàn lived in Campbell country he fought against the Jacobite clans at Culloden, but like many Highlanders of his day, he had little choice. Under the clan system, you followed your chief into battle whether you liked it or not. But Duncan Bàn's later poems show strong Jacobite sympathies and he was among the first to decry the depopulation of the Highlands and the dispersal of the Gaels.

He had a long and adventurous life after leaving his native glen, serving in the Breadalbane Fencibles and eventually in the Edinburgh City Guard, the forerunner of the modern police force.

He is buried in the famous Greyfriars Churchyard in Edinburgh where an imposing monument, erected by his admirers, marks his grave.

As Archibald, Duke of Argyll, a Gaelic scholar and the grandfather of the present duke, once said: "Robert Burns, Scotland's national bard, undoubtedly merits his reputation as one of the world's great poets, but we Gaels also have our own bard and his name is Duncan Bàn Macintyre."

John MacLeod of Glen Nevis here lent me a book of Duncan Bàn's poetry. The Gaelic translator and editor of the book, George Calder, says of Macintyre:

> His poetical talents justly entitle him to rank among the first bards of the world, for all good judges of Celtic poetry agree that nothing like the purity of his Gaelic and the style of his poetry has appeared in the Highlands of Scotland since the days of his countryman, the sublime Ossian.

Mr. Calder might be guilty of some Victorian exaggeration, considering the fact that over 1,400 years separate the legendary Ossian from Duncan Bàn and there were many fine Gaelic poets during those years, but in output alone (over 100 of his poems have been published), he was without an equal. His most famous poem *In Praise of Ben Dorain* covers 30 pages and is still at the top of the Gaelic Hit Parade.

On a hill by the side of the road near Dalmally, Loch Awe, is a monument to Duncan Bàn. Many years ago Anne and I climbed up to it and looked around at the majestic scenes that the poet loved so well and wrote about so touchingly. The deer are still there and can be readily seen in winter and spring in Glen Orchy before they leave to summer on the high mountains.

Although he was forester and gamekeeper to both the Earl of Breadalbane and the Duke of Argyll and stalking the red deer was part of his job, he never lost his love and respect for these magnificent beasts. His attitude to them was very much like the attitude of Canada's Native people to the caribou. They know that they must kill the animals to survive but they do not look down upon or despise them. If anything, they revere them and thank them and the Creator for their beauty and usefulness. In this more enlightened age of belief in the sanctity of life it may be difficult to understand the old attitudes. At least the life and death of a stag was attended with awe and respect.

> *'S binne na gach beus / Anail mhic an fhéidh / A' langanaich air eudan / Beinn-Dòrain.* And sweeter than all art / The breath of the son of the hart / Belling on steepest part / Of Ben Dorain

In Praise of Ben Dorain is composed in the form of a *piobaireachd*, (pronounced pee-broch). Properly called *ceòl-mòr*, (kyole-more), it is what might be called the classical form of piping, consisting of a theme and variations, the rhythm flowing freely, as in a song. Duncan Bàn loved the pipes and composed many songs praising them. But his poetic genius extended to many other topics. His *Song to my Newly Wedded Wife* is a touching tribute to his loved one. It begins:

> *A Mhàiri bhàn òg, 's tu 'n òigh th'air m'aire, / Ri'm bheò bhi far am bithinn fhéin;* O fair young Mairi, thou's the maid I'm intending / To be where I am while I live...

An admirer of the poem, fascinated by the description of Duncan's wife, but disappointed by her actual appearance, hinted that she was not so very beautiful. Duncan gently reproved him: *"Cha n-fhaca tusa i leis na sùilean agamsa -* You have not seen her with *my* eyes," he said.

The late Marion MacMaster of Laggan had a note-book written by John MacMaster, a schoolteacher here in Glengarry about a century ago. In it he has lovingly inscribed, in a beautiful hand, many of the poems of Duncan Bàn. It is a treasured keepsake in the MacMaster family.

Dr. Charles Dunn, Gaelic Scholar

Mac-talla, "the son of the rock" — Gaelic for "echo"

As mentioned in the previous article, Dr. Charles Dunn of Harvard University's Department of Celtic Languages and Literature conducted a workshop at *Feis-Glengarry '94* which he called *Preserving the Highland Story.* At his request, the workshop was conducted in an easy-going, informal style, with Dr. Dunn reminiscing about a lifetime devoted to the study of the Celtic peoples and the Highland Gaels in particular.

Although his 1953 book *Highland Settler* is concerned mostly with the Maritimes, he does refer to Glengarry in it and came here to do research on several occasions. In 1962 Dr. Dunn wrote an article for *The Dalhousie Review*, called *Glengarry's Gaelic Heritage.* Here are some excerpts from it:

> Glengarry County and its local writers have profited mutually from one another. The county has supplied the colourful background of its Highland Scottish traditions. Its literary

publicists have in turn attached a special aura to the county. No other county in Canada, so far as I know ... has attained such status.

Dr. Dunn goes on to list Gaelic publications in the early days of Highland settlement in North America. That there was any printed Gaelic at all in the New World was quite remarkable, as for most, Gaelic was a spoken language, not a written one, and many could not read or write it.

But there must have been some, nevertheless, who could appreciate the written word, or perhaps could have it read to them, because Dr. Dunn lists Gaelic publications from as early as 1791 (from North Carolina), and later from Prince Edward Island, from Nova Scotia and from Montreal. In Ontario the earliest Gaelic publications seem to have been *Cuartair na Coille* (The Forest Traveller), published at Kingston in 1840 and 1841, and another called *Am Fear-Teagaisg* (The Teacher), published, as he says,

> ...at some unspecified locality, also in Ontario, in 1850. No surviving copies of these ephemeral works have as yet been found, but they may still be lurking in some Glengarry attic.... The earliest Gaelic publication known to have originated in Glengarry is apparently *An Teagasg Chriosd* (The Teaching of Christ), a catechism prepared by the Rev. John MacDonald, Vicar-General of Alexandria. It was printed in 1871.

> Local newspapers such as *The Glengarry Review* (1884-1888) and *The Glengarrian* carried some Gaelic articles.

> Dr. MacDiarmid of Maxville (a dentist) ran a series of Gaelic lessons in *The Glengarrian.* Dr. D.D. MacDonald of Alexandria, among others, provided Gaelic songs.

Local research has turned up about 17 other Glengarry Gaelic poets who wrote for various publications between 1890 and 1905 alone. The Highland Society is in the process of identifying them.

> Occasionally, also, some writer who understood Gaelic culture as an insider would produce an invaluable study of the Glengarry tradition. J.A.Macdonell (Greenfield) first published his important *Sketches Illustrating the Early Settlement of Glengarry in Canada* in *The Glengarrian* (in English) in 1889. George Sandfield Macdonald wrote on the county's literary background in *The Transactions of the Celtic Society* of Montreal 1887. Miss C.A.Fraser published a paper on Glengarry folk tales in the

Journal of American Folklore (1893). John MacLennan, MP, Lancaster, wrote an historical sketch entitled *The Early Settlement of Glengarry,* which is now preserved in manuscript in the Public Archives of Ontario.

During the last quarter of the nineteenth century Glengarrians were in contact, moreover, with Gaelic literary journals of a wider sphere. Angus Nicholson began publishing *An Gaidheal* (The Gael) in Toronto in 1871 and appointed agencies in Williamstown and Finch. Later, Jonathan G. MacKinnon of Cape Breton published his excellent and readable journal *MacTalla* (Echo) in Sydney (1892-1904) and attracted numerous and enthusiastic subscribers from Glengarry and its vicinity.

I remember as a child in Montreal, my aunt Rose McKenna reading *MacTalla* and *The Antigonish Casket*, with its Gaelic columns, sent to her from our cousin, the mother of Mary McIntyre of Lancaster.

In *MacTalla* one year, Jonathan MacKinnon recorded a trip that he had made to Prince Edward Island to see if any of the large Highland population there still spoke Gaelic. Sadly, he reported that those he met no longer spoke it, and, in his words, "had found nothing better in its place."

The Lion's Tongue

Language is the dress of thought — Samuel Johnson

Some menus and programmes from Burns' Night Suppers and St Andrew's Day celebrations of a few generations ago in Greater Glengarry were recently donated to the Glengarry Highland Society.

It is only fitting that the Burns' Night programme should be devoted to the songs and poems of the Scottish Lowlands, although unless one were a native speaker of the Lowland tongue (and there were very few in this area) it would be hard to believe that any Glengarrians could understand, then or now, what *"baps an' dabs on a whang"* or *"bubbly jocks wi' fattrills"* or a *"willie-waught"* meant on the menu. But it was quite proper for a Burns' Night Supper because Robert Burns was a Lowland Scot and should be honoured as such, and Lallans, the Lowland tongue, not Gaelic, was his language.

It is when we come to the St Andrew's Day banquets that the mind boggles. In this Highland heart of Ontario, where so many had Gaelic as their mother tongue, the 1933 annual banquet of the St Andrew's Society of Cornwall featured songs like *Old MacDonald Had a Farm* and *Love's Old Sweet Song*. Where were the great Gaelic songs that were the heritage of the Highland people? Not one is on the list. Where was the Lion's Tongue, as poets described Gaelic, honoured on that day? Not at these St Andrew's Day celebrations, at any rate. It's as if the language of the Highland Scots, one of the world's oldest and most beautiful tongues, had never existed — and this within a stone's throw of the residence of John Sandfield Macdonald, the first premier of Ontario, who spoke Gaelic before he spoke English and who many believe was as great a Canadian as our country's first prime minister Sir John A. MacDonald. John A. also knew Gaelic, as did Canada's second prime minister Sir Alexander MacKenzie, as well as the first attorney-general of Ontario and most of the elected officials from this area in the early days. Why is Gaelic so rarely heard now?

Scotland was united as a nation in the ninth century under Kenneth MacAlpin. The Gaelic-speaking King of Scots, Malcolm Canmore, married, in the twelfth century, the English-speaking woman who became St Margaret of Scotland. She was undoubtedly a saintly woman as were several of her children, but she was determined to replace Gaelic with English at the Scottish court. And as the court goes, so goes the nation; Gaelic and the culture of the Highland Scots gradually declined and an alien culture eventually took its place.

Within a few centuries, Gaelic was confined to the more remote areas of the Highlands. Among those areas were the ancestral homes of the people of Glengarry.

Although English may have become the language of the aristocracy, the people of the Lowlands spoke their own version of it, a language as old as English and derived from many of the same sources, Low German, Friesian, Saxon, and the Scandinavian tongues. Variously called Lallans, Doric, or Scots, it was spoken throughout non-Gaelic Scotland. In its pure form it is now obsolete, and most Scots now speak a diluted version, mistakenly regarded by some as English with a Scottish accent. It is more correctly a modern form of the old Scots tongue.

As the population of the Lowlands exploded from the seventeenth century on and the Gaelic-speaking people declined, the proportion of the population speaking Gaelic decreased until today it is spoken by less than two percent of the inhabitants of Scotland.

But what of the Gaelic language in Glengarry? From the everyday tongue of about twenty thousand here for the better part of two centuries, it is now reduced to a fond memory, understood by a few senior citizens and spoken only at the Gaelic classes sponsored by the Highland Society.

It is easy to blame the loss of the language on the natural evolution of the population into the English-speaking world of the North American majority; it is only in the last generation or so that the idea that children could easily learn two or more languages before the age of twelve has been realized. That idea is still not accepted by everyone.

The old perception was that a second language introduced too early in life would be confusing, and neither would be spoken properly. Dr. Wilder Penfield, of Montreal Neurological Institute fame, claimed that a child could acquire other languages without any difficulty if learned through the ear, as the mother tongue is learned.

Millions of Europeans speak several languages other than their own and think nothing of it. But they are encouraged to acquire other languages. In Canada, the learning of a language other than French or English is often considered eccentric, if not plain suspicious.

It is true that as a rule the language of the majority in a community or a country prevails but we now know that fluency in the majority tongue can easily be accompanied by a knowledge of more than one other. In the case of the descendants of the Highland Scots who settled here, that other language could be Gaelic. It need not interfere with the learning of English and French, and would be a source of interest and pleasure to those who are proud of their heritage.

No one would suggest that Gaelic should or could be spoken fluently again here as a daily language. Those days are gone. But as the classical forms of Latin and Greek which have little relevance to most Canadians have been dropped from schools, it seems reasonable to suggest that in an area such as Glengarry, where Gaelic was the language of the people within living memory, a knowledge of it should form part of a Canadian heritage course.

Attitude is the important thing. If the prevailing attitude is "why bother? It's of no use in the modern world," or "we have enough to learn without adding more difficulties," the response could be: "Becoming familiar with some basic Gaelic is easy if taught properly. Fluency is not necessary. Appreciation is."

If Gaelic dies out we will lose something of great beauty and value. It was the language of our ancestors for countless generations. It was the language spoken by them as they cleared the land for their children. It was spoken by those brave and hardy men and women who helped build this

on't know how they were tuned, how they really sounded,
se the last *clarsair*, the last man to play the clarsach in the
ional way, died almost two hundred years ago, taking the
t with him to the grave.

ning, however, believes that by the 16th century

s tuned chromatically, unlike the European harp, which was a
le diatonically tuned instrument. It is likely that the clarsach
uned, at least partly, chromatically, since very early times.

lem is that once the strings were loosened or broken and no
alive to tune it properly, and no written words survived to de-
do it, the secret was lost forever. If the Great Highland Bag-
sed being played 200 years ago, the scale of the chanter could
ately reproduced today by fitting a reed to one of the chanters
t from the 18th century. The tone of wind instruments is set by
e finger holes, but the tone of stringed instruments must be set
g or loosening each individual string, as in a violin or guitar,
ern instruments are now tuned to the same scale. But the Gael,
often said, was (and sometimes still is), different, and that dif-
ies through the music as well.

akes the Highland bagpipe so popular today is that strange, al-
al sound, caused by the slightly different notes of the chanter. It
nform exactly to the accepted scale of the other musical instru-
e European mode, and that difference would have been apparent
ach as well.

rsach was much smaller than the modern concert harp, as can be
those preserved in museums. It was often decorated with the
iful and intricate Celtic designs. John Downing again:

e sound of the clarsach, according to the writings of foreign
servers, was prolonged, resounding, and sweet in tone. The
fficulty of playing the clarsach was greatly increased by its
mplex tuning and the need to damp the prolonged sound of the
rings with the fingers, when necessary, to avoid inharmonious
und clashes. By the 16th century, the sound of the clarsach had
ecome much admired in Europe and Irish harpers were often to be
en performing in the royal courts and households of England,
ermany, Denmark and Italy.

he fingernails of the harper were grown long, shaped like plectra
nd used to strike the strings. As late as the 18th century we learn
f one Eichlin O'Kane, by all accounts an accomplished musician,

country, by Simon Fraser, Alexander MacKenzie, Spanish John McDonell, the Rev. John Bethune and the Big Bishop, Alexander Macdonell.

Finnan the Buffalo McDonald, who earned his nickname by wrestling a maddened bull buffalo to a standstill, had little formal education but spoke Gaelic, English, French, and several Native languages. Why is a knowledge of Gaelic considered so difficult? It belongs to us all. It is part of Canada's heritage.

There are many misconceptions about Gaelic: That it is a dead language, that it has no words for modern terms, and so on. Gaelic may have been losing ground for centuries, but it is far from dead. There are about 100,000 people who still speak it in Scotland. About half of them speak it as their daily language. As to not having any modern words, Gaelic borrows from other languages just as English has always done. Over half the words in the English dictionary come from Latin, Greek, French, and dozens of other tongues.

Some years ago there was opposition in Scotland to the use of the original Gaelic on road signs in Gaelic-speaking areas. There was no question of having unilingual signs, but many people in the Highlands felt that Gaelic should at least be recognized as much as any other language. An anti-Gaelic attitude was particularly virulent among many of the outsiders who had taken up residence in what they probably considered simply an extension of their native places of Glasgow, Liverpool or Manchester.

At a meeting of the Inverness County Council in the 1960s, a retired army officer from the south was particularly scathing in his opposition to the use of Gaelic on road signs. "It's a dead language," he blustered, "it has no modern words!" The man who told us this story was also a member of the council and a fluent Gaelic speaker. He knew that the remark was directed at him. "Give us an example, Colonel, of an English word that has no Gaelic equivalent," he responded. The Colonel thought deeply. "Aha!" he finally said, "I've got you! How do you say spaghetti in Gaelic?" "How do you say it in English?" said our friend.

In the early days in Glengarry those moving away to work in the city were often humiliated when their English was not fluent. Sometimes even their soft Gaelic accents, (so different from the more guttural Lowland speech of the non-Gaelic Scots), were mocked by city folk. Such experiences were often enough to turn them against their mother tongue. Some couldn't wait to forget their heritage and become part of what they considered a more attractive culture.

Dr. C.M.C. Smelt of Cornwall, Ontario, learned Gaelic when he was a student in Scotland. There he heard the sad story of how one family lost their Gaelic. It was told to him by one of the children involved. One evening at the table, their father interrupted their conversation in Gaelic, struck his fist on the table and shouted: "You will never again speak that language in this house. It will never do you any good in this world. It is a useless language and worth nothing to you!" And so shame and guilt were heaped on the children for speaking their mother tongue. Variations of this behaviour, usually in more subtle ways, were a major cause of the loss of the lion's tongue.

Unfortunately, many Gaels themselves believed the calumnies of their enemies, that Gaelic was inferior, a gibberish, a rough and savage tongue. They were ignorant of the long history of Gaelic, which was spoken for centuries before English, French, or other modern European languages evolved. They were ignorant of the poems and songs of the Gael and the thrilling and heart-rending beauty of Scots Highland music.

Some years ago at Mòd-Ontario, the Gaelic festival in Toronto, Simon MacKenzie, a guest artist from Scotland, sang a bardic song that had been traced back at least nine hundred years, representing the oldest living folk tradition of the Western World.

ᕼarps

No harp like my own could so cheerily play —
Thomas Campbell 1777-1844

The harp is the musical symbol of Scotland, Ireland and Wales and John Downing of the Eigg Road is an expert on harps.

John is an Englishman and a native of Oxford and has had a life-long interest in music. Although he does not play the harp, he does play the lute, first cousin to the harp, and has constructed a Celtic harp which has been on display at the Museum of Civilization. I am indebted to him for much of the information in this column.

The origins of the harp go back to the earliest recorded times. All stringed instruments, lyre, lute, clavichord, violin, guitar, and hundreds of others are related. They are played by striking, stroking, strumming or plucking strings made of gut or metal which are tuned to the desired pitch by being tightened or loosened. We know that King David played a harp-like instrument and carvings of harpers are found on ancient monuments dating back thousands of years throughout the Mediterranean world and beyond.

It is John Downing's belief th
when they migrated into Europe fr
the British Isles and Ireland, the Ce
rope, but unlike the Greeks and I
Their culture was an oral one and al
the early Christian era, they persist

According to Latin writers, the
them, could perform prodigious feat
sands of lines of heroic verse at a tin
and legend, was passed on from lip t
gree of intellectual ability, but as th
curred in their way of life, and as virtu
was irretrievably lost.

So it was with their music, and th
ments.

To try to understand the history o
must go back over two thousand year
aries, as we know them, existed. In We
man Empire and tribal societies w
Alliances were based more on languag
ral that the Gaelic-speaking Celts of Ire
Antrim at the beginning of the Christia
was later to become Scotland considere
to an extension of their Irish world, isol

As their language came with them, s
it remained that way for the better part ol
ural that there would have been great c
Gaelic people. There are only a few se
Scotland, and local chiefs in both areas
musicians crossing back and forth, sharir
Thus the harp came to Scotland.

To quote John Downing:

> The clarsach was an instrument u
> European counterparts. About a do
> various states of disrepair includir
> Queen Mary harp and the Lamon
> National Museum of Scotland in E

But there is one enormous problem v
plained to me:

having performed before the courts of Europe, the pope and the exiled Stuart king, but lacking in social skills. One evening, while performing in Scotland, he was most offensive to his hosts. When his insolence could no longer be overlooked, the Highland gentlemen ordered his fingernails to be cut short before sending him from their house — a sufficient punishment as he was then unable to play upon the harp again until they had grown back!

The eclipse of the Irish harp became complete with the transcription of the old harp music of Ireland and Scotland into a new form suitable for the violin and piano. The music thus lost its identity so that we are now unable to say for certain which of the traditional melodies of both countries that we hear today was originally performed on the clarsach, either in its ancient or later forms.

One of the last hereditary *clarsair* in Scotland appears to have been Murdoch MacDonald, harper to MacLean of Coll, who died at an advanced age in 1739. During the next few generations, the clarsach gradually was replaced by other stringed instruments, the harpsichord and, eventually, the piano.

The Kintail Bard

Fair the fall of songs / When the singer sings them
— Robert Louis Stevenson

Muriel Aitken is a member of our Glengarry Gaelic Choir. She is also a soloist, and one of the most beautiful songs she sings is *Dean Cadalan Samhach* — Sleep Softly, by the Kintail Bard John Macrae.

Sister Margaret MacDonell in her 1982 book *The Emigrant Experience* quotes the song, in Gaelic and English, and states that it was probably addressed to the bard's daughter after they had emigrated to North Carolina around 1774.

The poem, as the title suggests, was composed to comfort the bard's family in the New World, where everything was so different from the Highland home that they had left with such sadness:

Dean cadalan sàmhach, a chuilean mo rùin; / Dean fuireach mar tha thu, 's tu an dràsd' an àit' ùr. Sleep softly, my darling beloved; /Stay as you are, now that you are in a new land.

But as he tries to console his loved one and give her hope for the future, he can't help but compare their former life in Kintail to "the never-ending forest" of 18th century America.

> Bear my farewell and greeting to Kintail of the cattle, / where I spent my time when I was a young child. / There dark-haired lads would dance heel and toe to the music / with girls with flowing tresses and cheeks like roses.

This nostalgia for their homeland was shared by many of the early Highland settlers. They called it *cianalas*, which can be translated as "homesickness" but in the Gaelic it means far more than that. It is a melancholy, a sadness and a loneliness which sometimes descends into a terrible heartsickness and depression from which the sufferer never completely recovers.

The reality in those days was that conditions in the Highlands had become so unbearable in the years after Culloden that emigration for many had become not a choice, but a necessity, regardless of the heartbreak involved.

The Kintail bard is known as John Macrae in English but in the large glen that is Kintail, where almost all were Macraes, he was known as *Iain MacMhurchaidh*, John, Son of Murdoch.

He apparently belonged to a family known for generations for their learning and poetry, and was greatly respected throughout the area, from the Chisholm lands of Strathglass which border Kintail on the north to the neighbouring lands of the MacDonells of Glengarry to the south and to the Isle of Skye to the west.

When the bard decided to leave his native land with his family for America, many tried to dissuade him, but he had made up his mind. The old Gaelic way of life was no more and the chiefs who traditionally supported the bards had become nothing but landlords, with little feeling for the ancient language of their race or for the poets who sang in it. As he says in another Gaelic poem, traditionally said to have been inspired by a letter from John Bethune, the Presbyterian minister who was already in North Carolina:

> Let us go and may God's blessing be with us. / Let us go and charter a vessel. / Better than to remain under landlords / who will not tolerate tenantry; / who would prefer gold to a brave man, though it would be in a crab's claw; / who would prefer instead of a handsome hero / the bandy-legged cheat with his wealth.

The grasping crab was the symbol of greediness and meanness which the open-handed Highlanders despised.

John Macrae was a royalist and opposed the rebels in North Carolina. In the tradition of the Celtic bards whose persons were sacred and inviolate, he fearlessly spoke out. He knew what horrors had been perpetrated against his people in the Highlands by the government after Culloden and evidently thought that the rebels in North Carolina would fail and suffer the same fate.

But the Americans knew nothing of the sanctity of Gaelic poets. They seized his property and threw him into prison, finally killing him, some believe, by tying him to two horses and driving them in opposite directions.

Nothing is known of the fate of his family as far as I can discover. All that remains are his songs.

His friend John Bethune was also imprisoned in North Carolina but released. He came to Montreal and founded the St Gabriel Street Presbyterian church there. Hearing that there was need of a minister in Glengarry, he came here with his family. Two centuries later, the Glengarry Gaelic Choir sang the Kintail bard's song about the letter from John Bethune in the Bethune -Thompson house in Williamstown where the minister and his family once lived.

SO A MHIC! ✴

CIAMAR A THA D'UAIREADAIR?

Ma tha e am feum caraidh
air doigh sam bith, thoir gu

Fionnladh T. Rothach

Seudair agus Uaireadairiche.
Uaireadairean Oir us Airgid agus
Seudan dhe gach seorsa..
Uaireadairean air an glanadh 's air an caradh

Agus theid mi an urras air an obair.

F. T. MUNRO, Watchmaker & Jeweller,
MAXVILLE, ONT.

Advertisement from The Glengarry News, 1896. Notices such as this appeared in Gaelic-speaking areas in Nova Scotia and Glengarry a century ago. The translation is: *Here sons! How is your watch? If it is in need of repair in any way, give it to Finlay T. Munro, jeweller and watchmaker. Gold and silver watches and jewels of every sort. Watches cleaned and repaired. And I will guarantee the work.*

Glengarry Clans, Families and Local Heroes

Who was MacBeth?

Brave MacBeth, - well he deserves that name — Shakespeare

OUR GRANDSON Michael Sandy studied Shakespeare's MacBeth in school last year. Someone told him that MacBeth never really existed. He was able to correct that idea; MacBeth was King of Scots in the 11th century, but the historical MacBeth bears little resemblance to Shakespeare's king.

MacBeth did indeed murder King Duncan in 1040 and seize the throne, not an uncommon practice in those days and not confined to Scotland, but he seems to have had a change of heart afterwards. Mackenzie, in *A Short History of the Highlands and Islands,* says:

> The use he made of his acquired power —— was generally for the good of his country; while his character, far from being irresolute, was marked by vigour and ability. He was the friend of the poor, the protector of the monks, and the first Scottish king whose name appears in ecclesiastical records as a benefactor of the Church.

In Gaelic, which was his mother tongue, MacBeth would have spelled his name *Macbethad,* in modern Gaelic *Macbeatha,* (son of life, a religious person, one of the elect). As time went on the name also became anglicized as Beaton or Bethune, and to further complicate matters, in Skye it was sometimes spelled Peutan, which makes sense because in Gaelic *b* is usually pronounced softly, more like *p*. We first came upon this soft Gaelic b many years ago. Bob Hannah was Pipe-Major of the Montreal Black Watch. His wife Annie, a native Gaelic speaker, referred to him as Pop, or so we thought; it seemed a strange way for a dignified Highland woman to refer to her husband until we realized that she was saying Bob with the Gaelic soft *b*.

In Cape Breton the spelling Beaton seems to be preferred, while here in Glengarry Bethune is usual. Both versions are pronounced by Gaelic speakers as BAY-tin. I was told recently by a neighbour here in Glengarry that his grandmother would be very annoyed if the traditional Gaelic pronunciation of their family name was used. She evidently thought that Bethune sounded fancier.

The most famous Bethune in the early days of Glengarry was the Presbyterian minister, Rev. John Bethune. He was a native of the Isle of Skye who came to North Carolina and ministered there until the American Revolution forced him out.

Bethune came to Montreal where he established the St Gabriel Street Presbyterian Church. Before that church was built, the congregation was invited by the Recollet Fathers to use their church for divine service. This example of Christian co-operation followed Bethune when he settled in Glengarry, where he and his wife spent the rest of their lives and raised a large family.

John Bethune became the close friend of Alexander Macdonell, the Highland priest who eventually became the first bishop of Upper Canada and lived at St Raphael's, a short distance from the Bethune home in Williamstown, and they evidently shared many happy visits.

As the only Presbyterian minister in the early days in Glengarry, Bethune was helped by Macdonell when he himself was unavailable to attend at the bedside of a sick or dying member of his congregation. The priest would often take the minister's place, using the Presbyterian prayers he had learned as a child in Scotland from his mother. When a dispute broke out at one point between Bethune and the elders of Williamstown Presbyterian Church, the Big Bishop was asked to arbitrate. His decision was accepted.

We have no way of knowing if John Bethune had any connection with MacBeth, but we do know that the Bethunes were hereditary physicians to the MacDonald Lords of the Isles for centuries, and we know that many of John Bethune's numerous family achieved renown.

One of his descendants was Dr. Norman Bethune, "the hero of Red China" and one of the most honoured foreign names in modern China, who died of blood poisoning while looking after the wounded during the Long March in the 1940s. Dr. Bethune may not have been aware of it, but the tradition of healing in his family stretched back over eight hundred years.

The MacGillivrays

The clan of the cat

All Highland clans had a seat, a castle or stronghold where the chief lived. Some of the more powerful clans such as the MacDonalds had many castles at various times from which the chief or sub-chiefs dispensed justice and settled disputes.

The MacGillivray castle is Dunmaglas in Strathnairn near Inverness. Culloden is nearby. On that sad and dismal battlefield are many rough stone memorials, erected many years after the event which ended the old Highland way of life and eventually resulted in the destruction of the clan system. One of those stones is inscribed *the well of the dead where the chief of the MacGillivrays fell.*

There are many MacGillivrays in Greater Glengarry, particularly in the Glenelg - Kirkhill area of Lochiel Township (now North Glengarry).

MacGillivray, *MacGille-bhrath* in Gaelic, means *son of the servant of judgement.* It probably refers to a progenitor who was connected with the ancient Celtic legal system which governed the Gaelic world, based on the Brehon laws of tanistry. In later times the tanist or thane, an interpreter of the law or judge, became an important title, as in Shakespeare's MacBeth, where the three witches tell him that he will become Thane of Cawdor. The present head of the Campbell of Cawdor family has that title in his pedigree.

Clan MacGillivray was a member of Clan Chattan, a confederation of smaller clans united for mutual protection. It can be compared to the Iroquois League of the Six Nations which was established for much the same reason. Here is how Clan Chattan is described in *Collins Encyclopaedia of Scotland:*

> The original clan was probably descended from Gillechattan Mór, servant of St Chattan, living at Torcastle in Lochaber. In 1291 Angus, Chief of Mackintosh, married Eva, the Chattan chief's daughter, and he inherited the chiefship. But Clan Chattan in the 14th and later centuries was not of the same composition or character as the prehistoric clan. It became a confederation of (a) descendants of the original clan (MacPhersons, Cattanachs, Macbeans, Macphails), (b) Mackintoshes and their offshoots (Shaws, Farquharsons, Ritchies, McCombies, MacThomases) and

(c) families not originally related by blood (Macgillivrays, Davidsons, Macleans of Dochgarroch, MacQueens of Pollochaig, Macintyres of Badenoch, Macandrews). For over 600 years the Chief of Clan Mackintosh was also Chief or Captain of Clan Chattan.

The origin of the MacGillivrays before they settled in Strathnairn was on the Isle of Mull and in Morven on the adjoining mainland.

When Sir William MacGillivray, "The Lord of the Northwest," brother to Simon MacGillivray and nephew of Simon MacTavish of the North West Company retired as one of Canada's wealthiest men, he bought some of the ancient clan lands at Pennyghael in Mull. MacGillivray died before he could take possession of Pennyghael House, but his daughter, who was married to a man called Auldjo, lived there for many years with her family.

Glengarry Historian David Anderson tells me that the Auldjos of London were prominent Montreal merchants to the fur trade and Maitland, Garden, & Auldjo were Bishop Macdonell's bankers.

Although the Auldjos occupied Pennyghael House in the early part of the last century, almost two hundred years ago, some of the people who live in that part of Mull still tell stories about them. When in Mull some years ago, we visited our friend Duncan Lamont, a fine piper who lived on the Pennyghael estate. We viewed the Big House, now a shooting lodge owned by strangers, and returned to Duncan's croft house for tea. He produced and played a violin that his great-grandfather had made from driftwood and smoothed with a piece of broken glass. "He was a good player," said Duncan, "and he lived on the other side of that hill over there. He often was asked to play for the people at Pennyghael House, and they liked his playing so much that they gave him this house so that he would be closer to them. Their name was Auldjo."

So the twisted Highland paths that led from Mull to Culloden, to Canada and the founding of a nation, lead back to the hills of Pennyghael and the violin that William MacGillivray's daughter danced to so long ago.

Bill MacGillivray's Arm

An interview with a remarkable man

Bill MacGillivray of Kirkhill (Glenelg) here in Glengarry had two arms until he was 16 years old. Then his right arm was amputated at the shoulder. He was right-handed and had to learn how to use one hand instead of two. "Did it ever get you down — did you ever despair?" I asked him recently in the kitchen of his farmhouse. "Sometimes I got pretty frustrated," he said, "but I never gave up. I'm sort of stubborn, I think I got that from my mother's people. She was a MacLeod!" His eyes sparkled as he thought about what his late mother would have said about that.

When he still had two arms, Bill wanted to play lacrosse for the local Alexandria team, but it cost 25 cents a week to play. It was during the Depression of the Dirty Thirties and cash was scarce, so he made a deal with a neighbour who needed help. Bill and his dog would take the cows out to pasture twice a day, morning and evening, for 5 cents. At the end of the week he had 35 cents, enough to play lacrosse with a dime left over for all the luxuries a boy might want.

Before he lost his arm, Bill was a promising artist. He recently donated some of his early sketches to Marion MacMaster and she used them in her book on Glengarry Schoolhouses. But he never drew again after the age of sixteen. He directed his artistic abilities into the making of furniture in his workshop, which has several of Bill's inventions making it possible for a one-armed man to use power tools. He also rigged up a gadget to hold his fishing pole to allow him to use the reel. "I caught the biggest fish ever recorded in this area with it," he proudly says.

As well as operating his 200 acre farm (using only horses originally), he drives a tractor and pick-up truck. He has always supplied all the stovewood for the house, which he cuts in the bush at the back of his farm with a chainsaw. He has fixed up the saw with a special throttle cut-off which he made himself, and designed a board to support the saw when he uses it.

On New Year's Day, 1991, Bill had nothing much to do, as he says, so he decided to go to the bush and cut some wood. All alone as usual, he was doing very well until a tree fell the wrong way and broke his leg. "It wasn't satisfied with that" says Bill, "so it bounced back and hit me in the chest. I thought all my ribs were broken." He somehow crawled to his tractor, which was a few hundred feet away, got the clutch down with the uninjured leg (the one on the wrong side — he had broken his left leg) and drove home. "That was the easy part" says Bill. When he pulled up at the house, he fell off onto the verandah.

Wife Janet, son Jim, and grandson Michael got him inside. "That's when I began to shake" he says. "I couldn't stop." After a stay in the hospital, Bill came home and broke the same leg again, but in a different place. "I feel fine now," he says. "The important thing is never to give up. If you get knocked down, get up and keep swinging. Never admit defeat."

Bill says that the loss of his arm may well have prolonged his life. "I was fascinated with flying as a boy. I would certainly have joined the Air Force when war broke out if I had had my two arms and probably been killed, like so many of the young fellows from around here. As it is, I've had a long and satisfying life. I've done just about everything I ever wanted to do."

Bill doesn't want to be portrayed as a hero, but he's one just the same. True courage is not only displayed on the battlefield. It often goes unnoticed among our neighbours and friends.

The Chief of the MacGillivrays at the Battle of Culloden in 1746, the "Big Blacksmith" who fell, as they say in the Highlands, "with his face to the foe" would be proud of Bill MacGillivray. Then again, he might well say, if we could hear him speak, "what else would you expect of a MacGillivray — and a MacLeod as well?"

Mrs. Angus George

The road to a friend's house is never long — Proverb

Lilian George is the widow of the great athlete from St Regis, Angus George, whose memory is enshrined in the Glengarry Sports Hall of Fame. Although born on the Mohawk territory of Akwesasne, across the St Lawrence from Cornwall, Angus and Lilian lived for many years in the Glen Nevis area of Lancaster Township, Glengarry.

Angus gained his reputation as a superb lacrosse player. He and Lilian retired to St Regis some years ago, where he died.

David Anderson was president of The Glengarry Historical Society when we visited Lilian George at her home. She is a remarkable woman in her own right. She worked for Morgan's Department Store (now The Bay) in Montreal for many years and speaks Mohawk, English, and French.

The Mohawks of Awknesasne were famous for their handling of canoes on the rough waters of the St Lawrence and Lilian George's grandfather, she told us, was no exception. He was one of the skilled boatmen who helped sail the British Expeditionary Force up the Nile to the Sudan to battle the Mahdi's army at Khartoum at the end of the last century.

That strange Imperialist war ended with the Battle of Omdurman and the last full cavalry charge in British history. One of the subalterns who rode in that charge was the young Winston Churchill.

A century earlier, Mohawks had accompanied the Nor'Westers and the voyageurs in their trade canoes through the rivers and lakes of Canada to the Pacific.

The Mohawks were early allies of the British. That friendship was exemplified by the respect they had for Sir William Johnson of the Mohawk Valley and, after his death, for his son Sir John Johnson, who brought the first Highlanders to Glengarry. Without the support of the Mohawk nation Canada might never have survived.

Mrs. Angus George lives near the historic church of St Regis, which two centuries ago was in the care of Father Roderick Macdonell, a son of John Macdonell of Leek. (The Macdonells of Leek were tacksmen of MacDonell of Glengarry. *Leac* is the Gaelic for a flagstone or the summit of a hill.)

The Highlanders, and in particular the Nor'Westers, had much in common with the native people here and across Canada. The Gaelic-speaking Scots came from a culture that knew few luxuries. They were inured to hardship and could travel long distances when on military campaigns without cumbersome supply trains. They carried a small sack of oatmeal and a flat iron pan on which they would cook bonnach, the oatcake that sustained them. (Thus the word "bannock" came into native languages across North America for "bread.") The transition to the more nourishing pemmican of the western plains as a staple would have come easily to the Highlanders.

The legendary toughness of the Highlanders is illustrated by an anecdote, here credited to the Camerons, but claimed by several clans. A party of Lochaber men, forced to spend a wintry night in the open, rolled themselves in their plaids and lay down in the snow. One man made a large snowball on which to rest his head. The Cameron chief stomped over and kicked away the snow cushion. "Never let it be said," he roared, "that a Cameron needs a pillow!"

But it was when we spoke to Lilian George about some of the spiritual beliefs and traditions of her people that we recognized how close they were to the old Highland ways.

We asked her if she attended services at the St Regis Catholic church. "Sometimes," she said, "but I really follow the Traditional Way." She is a member of the Turtle Clan, and women of her standing wield a lot of authority in the Mohawk community. A person of great dignity and obvious wisdom, she is highly respected among the tribal leaders.

In *Carmina Gadelica*, that superb collection of Gaelic folklore first published one hundred years ago, Alexander Carmichael records prayers, incantations, rites, and customs, some going back to pre-Christian days. When we quoted some of these to Lilian, the prayers to the forces of nature, the blessings for sowing and reaping, and the unseen spirits that inhabit the Celtic world, she nodded her head. "We have many of the same things," she said, "but of course we have different names for them."

It is easy to understand how the early Highland people here, meeting the Natives for the first time, would have found common ground. We asked Lilian about "the little people" who appear so often in Gaelic lore: "Yes, we have them too," she said. "The other night some young people saw some in the woods near here. They were afraid and ran home. I told them they shouldn't have been afraid. Those spirits would never hurt you." And I'm sure they wouldn't, not with Mrs. Angus George around.

Stewarts and MacColls

Creag-an-Sgairbh — The Cormorant's Rock
— War cry of the Stewarts of Appin

Although today the word "steward" is just a fancy name for "waiter," it meant far more than that in the royal household of Scotland 700 years ago. The High Steward was in charge of all the monarch's possessions and supervised the operation of the royal court.

Walter, sixth High Steward of Scotland, married the daughter of Robert the Bruce in the 14th century and from them stems the Royal House of Stewart. When French was the language of the Scottish court, the name was spelled Steuart or Stuart, the latter spelling still preferred by many branches of the family. It is spelled *Stiùbhart* in Gaelic. It is pronounced the same way whatever the spelling.

Many noble families claim descent in the Stewart line, including those of Bute, Lennox, Athol, Albany (derived from the Gaelic name for Scotland, *Alba*) and a dozen more. In the Highlands they were assimilated into the Gaelic culture and became clans on their own, such as the Stewarts of Appin.

Appin borders Glencoe and extends south along the banks of Loch Linnhe to the MacDougall and Campbell lands of Lorn. Castle Stalker stands on a rocky islet opposite Portnacroish in Loch Linnhe. As its name implies, it was used by the Stewart kings as a hunting lodge for deer stalking. A ruin for centuries, it was recently restored and is occupied by a family which has Stewart connections. Although on a smaller scale, it attracts almost as many photographs as the better-known Eilean Donan Castle in Kintail.

On the mainland between Port Appin and Kentallen are several estates still occupied by Stuarts or Stewarts, attesting to the predominance of the name in the area.

The Stewarts of Appin were a small clan compared to their neighbours the Campbells, Camerons and MacDonalds, but they held their own for centuries in spite of their numbers. They were Jacobites, supporters of the House of Stewart and traditionally allied with the MacDonalds of Glencoe.

After the Massacre of Glencoe in 1692 many of the survivors made their way over the snow-covered mountains to sanctuary in Appin.

Some years after the defeat of the clans at Culloden in 1746 an Appin man, James Stewart of the Glen, was hanged for the murder of Colin Campbell of Glenure, an army officer who was hated by the Appin people for his cruel treatment of the Jacobite clans.

It is generally accepted that Stewart was not guilty of the crime and that the evidence at his trial was tainted. His remains were left to hang on the gibbet under an armed guard for months until his clansmen spirited away his bones for burial in an unmarked grave.

On a small hill where the gallows once stood, near the Ballachulish (pronounced Balla-hoo-lish) Hotel, is a memorial to James Stewart inscribed with the words "executed for a crime of which he was not guilty." The name of the actual perpetrator is said to be known to a family in the area but has never been revealed. The murder weapon, the "black gun of misfortune," is said to have been hidden in the thatched roof of a local cottage for years and has never been found.

Robert Louis Stevenson's *Kidnapped* is based on the Appin murder and is historically quite correct, except of course for the fictional story of David Balfour. The dashing adventurer Allan Breck (*breac*, pock-marked) Stewart, who befriends David in the book, was an actual person, a Jacobite agent who went secretly back and forth from France to Scotland, collecting a second tax from sympathetic Highlanders for the exiled Royal Stewarts.

Some say that Allan Breck was the murderer of Colin Campbell while others believe that it was a Cameron from Mamore in Lochaber, across the water from Ballachulish.

Highlanders began arriving in Glengarry in the 1780s and there were Appin Stewarts among them. If their descendants here know the true story of the Appin Murder they have never made it public.

The MacColls (*Col* was a fairly common first name, particularly among the MacDonalds) are an ancient clan who claim to have originated in Appin long before the Stewarts. The tradition of piping is particularly strong among them and in this century alone they have produced many fine pipers including the legendary John MacColl.

Many years ago I heard a story in Appin about a MacColl of another century. In the aftermath of Culloden as the British soldiers were bayoneting and cutting the throats of the wounded Jacobites, a young MacColl, the clan piper, searched the battlefield looking for his brother. He found him hidden in the heather, horribly mangled and unable to move. Knowing what would happen to him if he was captured, the severely wounded man begged his brother to finish him off. When the piper returned to Appin he never played the pipes again. He had no right hand.

The MacLeods

Skye, Glenelg, Harris and the Isle of Lewis

The Clan MacLeod is one of those Highland families which trace their origin to a Norse progenitor. *Leod* is the Gaelic form of the old Norse name *Liùtr* ® silent) and the man after whom the MacLeods are named was descended from Olav, King of the Isle of Man and the North Isles.

The Norsemen or Vikings began raiding Ireland and the British Isles in the 8th century.

> The Vikings owed their success to their invention of the keel, mastery of rudder and sail, and skill in navigation. This enabled them to make long sea journeys in their beautifully designed boats with effective forces of fighting men. In 794 they sacked Iona and returned in successive years to loot and murder. *Collins Encyclopaedia of Scotland.*

Other Highland clans claim descent from a Norse ancestor; the MacAulays (Olaf's son), the Morrisons, the MacSweyns (with all its variations, including MacQueen), the MacIvers, and the MacAskills. The MacDonalds are descended from Somerled, which in old Norse means "summer warrior." I don't think that there is a Highland clan that does not have a Viking or two in its genealogy.

It is not surprising that there is such a strong Norse influence in Gaelic Scotland. The Hebrides and much of the western mainland were under

Norse rule for centuries. Most of the old place names of the Isle of Lewis, the most northern of the Hebridean Islands, are Norse. But the Viking names and language were eventually swallowed up by the Gaelic majority, much as Gaelic eventually lost out to English.

The Clan MacLeod (*MacLeòid*) is divided into two main branches, the MacLeods of Dunvegan (Skye), Glenelg (on the mainland opposite Skye), and Harris (the southern part of the Isle of Lewis, considered a separate entity); and the MacLeods of Lewis, Waternish (Skye, but separate from Dunvegan) and Assynt (Sutherland).

In Gaelic, the first named are called *Siol Thormaid*, (the seed or descendants of Norman) and the other MacLeods are known as *Siol Thorcuil*, after Torquil, Norman's brother.

As in all Highland clans, feuds were the curse of their existence. During the 16th century in particular, the MacLeods fought with just about everybody, including those bearing the same name. The line of the MacLeods of Lewis became extinct and the MacLeods of the Isle of Raasay took over the leadership of *Siol Torquil.*

The most famous chief of the MacLeods of Dunvegan was Rory Mór, knighted by James VI of Scotland in 1603. P/M Colin MacLellan at a piping recital in Maxville a few years ago played two pibrochs (more properly called *ceòl mór*, the "great music") both composed by Patrick Mór MacCrimmon. The first was a salute to Rory Mór's birth, the second a lament on his death twenty-three years later. Rory Mór's drinking horn is still displayed in Dunvegan Castle.

The present chief, John MacLeod, the grandson of the renowned Dame Flora, visited here in Glengarry when his grandmother was the MacLeod chief and again when he became chief himself. He studied at McGill University and played in a ceilidh band while there. He also took part in the famous McGill production of *My Fur Lady*. At a reunion of the cast of the musical some years ago I talked with John MacLeod and he expressed great interest in his clanspeople in Glengarry.

In the summer of 1994 the Clan MacLeod Society of Glengarry and The Glenelg 1794 Committee sponsored a series of events commemorating the arrival of the Glenelg immigrants to Glengarry. It was a busy summer.

The MacArthurs

There is nothing older, unless the hills, MacArthur, and the devil
— Old proverb

This clan, *MacArtair* in Gaelic, is of very ancient origin, claiming to be the senior branch of Clan Campbell. They inhabited the lands of Strachur on Lochfyneside in Argyll from remote times. The clan supported Robert the Bruce in the 14th century in his successful struggle for Scottish independence, commemorated in the old song *Scots Wha Hae* and the modern popular tune *Flower of Scotland.*

The power of the MacArthurs waned at the start of the 15th century, and from then on the Campbells of Argyll became the leading clan in the region. Although a relatively small clan, the Argyll MacArthurs count among their more illustrious members John MacArthur of Australia "the Father of New South Wales" and General Douglas MacArthur, the military hero of the Pacific in World War II, who turned down the opportunity to run for president of the United States.

There was another family of MacArthurs in the Highlands in olden times who were hereditary pipers to the MacDonalds of the Isles. They had a college of piping on the Isle of Skye. They may not have had any connection with the Campbell MacArthurs (they spelled the name a little differently — *MacArtain*) and may have been simply descended from some other Arthur, which brings us to another difficulty in researching Gaelic names: We have to be careful about getting too dogmatic about them. There is no copyright on names, unless a name is taken for fraudulent purposes. To legally change a family name today one would have to follow a certain legal form, but that is a comparatively modern restriction and did not exist in olden times.

It was quite possible for the same name to crop up in more than one location and to have no connection. The only problems that might occur in a name change in those days would be questions of inheritance or clan pride. But as most Gaelic names derive from an illustrious ancestor's first name, and as there is no official registry of names as there is for ships or racehorses, there is nothing to say that there could not be two Hectors, for instance, in different places, to give their name to a clan — in this case, *MacEachain.*

Other common names, as in most languages, are related to trades, and most areas had a smith, *gobhainn*, whose son could rightly be called *Mac a' ghobainn*, MacGowan. The carpenter could give his name to a whole clan, as with Macintyre, *Mac an t-saoir*, the son of the carpenter, and there could be many of the same name without any blood connection.

In Scotland, shopkeepers selling tartans can produce a booklet for confused customers ostensibly proving that almost any name can be traced to a Highland origin. It's harmless, but not always correct. The reason that a name like Black, for example, might belong to Clan MacGregor is because the name MacGregor was outlawed in 1602 and members of that clan chose other names to hide their true identity. Some chose colours - Black, White, Blue, and so on but that doesn't mean that everyone who bears the name of a colour is a MacGregor (or a member of Clan Lamont, many of whom also chose colours to avoid trouble).

Colours in Gaelic are sometimes used to describe appearances — *Iain Dubh* (Ee-yun Doo), Black John, for someone with dark hair or a swarthy complexion, *fionn* (finn) for fair skin or hair, which became family names, as in Mickey Finn or Huckleberry Finn. Bàn means much the same, as in Donald Ban MacMaster or the family name Bain, MacBean or MacBain.

The Chisholms

Siosalach Strathghlais — Chisholm of the Green Valley

The Chisholms never seemed to have suffered from low self-esteem. Although a small clan, unlike their neighbours the MacKenzies and the Frasers who controlled large areas of the Highlands, the Chisholms were quite satisfied with Strathglass and Erchless Castle. But what a strath and what a castle!

Strathglass really lives up to its name — the green valley — and is one of the most verdant and fertile glens in the Highlands and Erchless Castle, hidden among the trees along the shore of the River Glass, is a beautifully preserved castle out of the past.

Unlike most of the glens of the Western Highlands, Strathglass and the area for miles around is well treed and the rich soil has generally produced strong, sturdy people.

The Chisholms and the MacRaes to the west in neighbouring, fertile, Kintail were often above average height. The Chisholms were reputed to have what the Lowlanders call "a guid conceit o' themsel's." It's not as bad as it sounds. "Conceit" in the old sense meant a sense of worth rather than false pride. The Chisholms knew that they were special and didn't pretend otherwise. How could they, when they were alleged to have believed that their chief was one of only three people in the world who was entitled to use the definite article: The Pope, The King, and The Chisholm!

The Highland Chisholms, like their Fraser neighbours, have non-Gaelic names, the Chisholms originating in the Lowlands and the Frasers in France. The progenitors of both clans seem to have moved into the Highlands some seven centuries ago, soon becoming, through marriage and assimilation, as Highland as any other clan.

The name Chisholm is *Sioslalach* in Gaelic, pronounced "Shiss-oh-lach," the "ch"sounded softly as in "loch." They were a warlike clan, often fighting against their neighbours in the feuds that were the curse of the Highlands. They were mostly strong Jacobites, supporters of the House of Stewart, and fought bravely at Culloden in 1746. Nothing illustrates the horror of Civil War more poignantly than the fact that the Chisholm chief and his son fought on opposite sides.

Long after the first Chisholms came to Glengarry and Cape Breton, those who remained in Strathglass were ruthlessly removed by their chief and there are few Chisholms left in their ancestral glen. Erchless Castle is now owned by others and the chief is long gone from the green valley.

In the Cape Breton segment of the award-winning video *The Blood is Strong*, the late Archie Chisholm, writer and local historian, is recorded as saying that as far as the Chisholms in Cape Breton are concerned, they would never accept the fact that their kinsmen were dispossessed by their own chief, although they indeed were. They share with many other Highlanders that pride of race that does not allow them to believe that they were ever betrayed by their chiefs.

The clan was loyal to Bonnie Prince Charlie during and after The '45 and a Chisholm was one of the Seven Men of Glenmoriston who saved his life after Culloden.

I have a reproduction of a picture of a Maj. Valentine Chisholm of The Black Watch, painted in Scotland over 200 years ago. His namesake was the secretary of Lochiel Township here in Glengarry for over 50 years. They look like doubles.

To the west of Glen Sandfield and in the area of St Andrew's West there are descendants of those Chisholms who came here from Strathglass. In the early days of the American West, a Chisholm blazed a trail that was used for cattle drives and by the pioneers moving west for generations, although the name is misspelled "Chisum" there.

Years ago, a woman here in Glengarry told me the story of how she had searched for her great-grandfather's last resting place in Strathglass. With the help of the local parish priest she searched through the burial records of the church, but to no avail. Finally, the priest asked her if she had inquired at the Presbyterian church nearby. "Oh no," she said, "he couldn't be there. All our family were staunch Catholics." "Well," said the priest, "sometimes during hard times it depended on who fed them." She found the grave in the Protestant graveyard.

The Macraes' Castle

Kintail, the home of the "Wild Macraes"

The most picturesque and most photographed castle in the Highlands of Scotland is *Eilean Donan* (pronounced "Ailen Dohnen") on Loch Duich in the area known as Kintail. It stands on a little rocky islet named after *Donan*, an early Celtic saint, and was held by the Macraes for their allies, the powerful MacKenzies, for centuries. Kintail, *Cinn-tàille*, the head of the sea, is a large glen surrounded by mountains. Most of the people living there two centuries ago were Macraes.

In the unsuccessful Jacobite Rising of 1719, Spanish troops joined the Macraes and some other clans in an attempt to return the Stewarts to the British throne. Eilean Donan castle, built in the 13th century, was blown up by the British and the countryside laid waste "to terrify the rebels" as the British General Wightman put it.

The castle remained a ruin for over two centuries. In the 1930s, Colonel Macrae-Gilstrap, a descendant of the Macraes who once were keepers of the castle, fulfilled a dream he had cherished since he was a child, and restored it to its former glory. He hired experts in architecture and masonry to make the re-built castle as authentic as possible. After years of work, Eilean Donan was ready to be lived in once again, the Macrae-Gilstraps moved in, and their descendants live there still — at least sometimes, because the castle is so cold, damp, and draughty that they can only stand it for brief periods of time.

Apart from the living quarters of the family, the castle is open to the public and visitors never cease to wonder at the care and obvious pains that have been taken to ensure that every detail of the construction is authentically correct — until Pierre Dussol arrived.

Pierre came to Canada from Argentina some years ago. His name originated in France and he is convinced that somewhere in his background, perhaps in the Scots Guards who served the French monarchy for centuries, he will find a Scottish ancestor. For Pierre is a Scotophile — he loves everything Scottish. He is a skilled craftsman, making full-sized replicas of ancient weapons as a hobby.

He recently brought one of his favourites, a huge two-handed sword, to one of the Highland Society's heritage classes at Glengarry District High School here in Alexandria. It is called a *claidheamh-dà-lamh* (clay da lav), or more commonly, a *claidheamh-mór*, (claymore), not to be confused with the basket-hilted broadsword, also called a claymore, worn in Highland regiments. This type of two-handed sword was used at the Battle of Bannockburn in 1314, but was gradually replaced by the smaller basket-hilted version over time. At about five or six feet in length, the two-handed sword, too long to wear at the waist, was carried on the back.

Pierre Dussol is a professional scene builder for stage productions and has worked on both sides of the Atlantic. He is also a piper, Gaelic learner, and an expert on the fortifications of the Middle Ages. He is built like a brick house himself and could probably wield the two-handed sword with ease. Few others could today. But it is in his capacity as an historian that he excelled on a recent visit to the Highlands.

Among the many castles that he visited was Eilean Donan. The guide there pointed out the ancient "yett," the defensive gate or door that was closed to hold back invaders. "It's upside down," said Pierre. "It opens the wrong way. The defenders, who would have had their swords in their right hands, could not have used them properly. And the yett is worn down only on the top — it should show scrape marks on the bottom, from rubbing along the stone floor." Pierre was right. The yett has since been re-hung.

Gunn and Forbes

In The Lochaber Emigrants to Glengarry, the book published a few years ago about Allan McMillan (Glenpean) and his cousin Archibald McMillan (Murlaggan), and the Highland people they brought to Glengarry and area in 1802, the ship's list is given. Naturally, most of the passengers' names begin with Mac or Mc, apart from a few like Campbell or Cameron, but there are a few that do not appear Highland at first glance, but which are, just the same. Gunn and Forbes are two of them.

The name Gunn, like Leod (*Ljót*) in MacLeod or Aulay (*Olaf*) in MacAulay, is of Scandinavian origin. Gunn is derived from the Norse first name Gunnar, and is *Guinne* in Gaelic. If your name is Gunn you belong to *Clan Gunnach*.

Many of the Norse-Gaelic clans claim descent from *Olaf*, King of the Isle of Man and the Hebrides in the 12th century. For centuries, the Western Isles, large areas of the northern mainland of Scotland and the islands of Orkney and Shetland were ruled from Norway.

Somerled, the half-Norse, half-Gaelic progenitor of Clan Donald, led the fight to expel the Norse from Scotland. In 1266, a century after his death, Norway finally gave up all claim to Scotland.

Although many family and place names remain to remind us of the Norse influence in the Highlands, and some Norse words entered Gaelic, the Norse language was swallowed up by the Gaelic majority and there is no evidence that any Scandinavian language was ever spoken in Scotland for any length of time.

The Gunns occupied lands in Caithness in the far north-east, *Gallaibh* in Gaelic, the "land of the stranger," showing the non-Gaelic origin of most of the people there. Caithness has strong connections with Orkney, and the eastern section is more Lowland than Highland.

The *Gàidhealtachd*, (pronounced "Gayl-tahkt"), the Gaelic-speaking Highlands, extends from the south-west of Kintyre to the far north-west of Sutherland and does not include the eastern part of Caithness. But 700 years ago, when almost all of Scotland was Gaelic-speaking, the Gunns considered themselves a Gaelic clan.

The Gunns are described in clan histories as "fierce, war-like, and ferocious," but what clan wasn't? They fought anybody and everybody, particularly the MacKays of Sutherland and the Keiths of Caithness. Some of the Gunns moved into MacKay territory and the feuds continued for centuries. Although never large in number, Clan Gunn held their own, sometimes against great odds.

The Forbes came from farther south in the Eastern Highlands of Aberdeenshire and take their name from the place there called Forbes. The present chief of the clan is descended from King Robert III and is the premier baron of Scotland.

Forbes was originally pronounced as two syllables — For-bess. When the new and present pronunciation became fashionable, it was said that it would "throw Lady Fettes (pronounced Fet-tes) into a Fit!" A piece of doggerel from that era survives;

> "...unsanctified snobs / That could mangle the sound of a fine Scottish name / And whittle it down into ... Fobbs!"

A branch of the clan produced Lord President Forbes of the Court of Session, a very influential Highlander who tried to prevent the clans from joining Bonnie Prince Charlie in 1745. Like many wise and knowledgeable men of the day, he knew that nothing would come of any Jacobite rising to restore the Stuarts but blood, misery, and defeat. He was right, but the hot-blooded Highlanders wouldn't listen. Many of the Forbes had joined the previous Jacobite Rising of 1715 and many were "out" again in The '45.

But it was too late for a successful outcome to such an ill-conceived Rising. Time had passed the Jacobites by. The vast majority of the people of Great Britain wanted peace and prosperity and an end to warfare.

It is a tragic irony of history that the defeat of the clans took place on the land of the man who had done his best to promote peace in the Highlands - Lord President Forbes of Culloden.

Ellice McDonald Jr. CBE

There is no joy without Clan Donald

I first met Ellice McDonald about 30 years ago when he and the late David Stewart of the Macdonald Tobacco Co. were organizing the Clan Donald Lands Trust. The then Lord Macdonald had died and his son and heir Godfrey, the present Lord Macdonald, was forced to sell most of his lands on the Isle of Skye to pay death duties.

Ellice McDonald had a dream, but unlike the case with most dreamers, he made his dream come true. He envisioned buying up about 20,000 acres of land from the Macdonald Estate and having it held in trust forever for the benefit of MacDonalds everywhere. His dream included setting up a Clan Donald Centre in the abandoned and mostly ruinous Armadale Castle on the Sleat (pronounced "Slate") peninsula, known as the "garden of Skye," because it was heavily treed from the days when the Macdonalds were wealthy and had turned the castle grounds into acres of flowers and shrubs.

Armadale Castle had been built in the early part of the 19th century, incorporating parts of a much older building, including the wing where Flora MacDonald, the saviour of Bonnie Prince Charlie, had stayed in 1746. By 1970, the older part of the castle was about all that was still standing, the more "modern" but badly-built 180-year old structure roofless and dangerous.

A lesser person would probably have given up when all the problems of setting-up and administering such an ambitious and grandiose scheme became apparent. But not Ellice. Over the years, with the support of David Stewart, Lord and Lady Macdonald, a wonderful Scots-American called Nestor MacDonald, and thousands of MacDonalds the world over, Ellice overcame every obstacle, and there were plenty. Over four million dollars have been invested so far in the Clan Donald Lands trust and the Clan Centre.

The broken-down part of the castle has been restored to a sculptured ruin, the Flora MacDonald section added to and turned into the finest Highland heritage centre in the world, and flats for visitors built within the walls.

H.L. Mencken, "The sage of Baltimore," was famous for his amusing observations on America as it was in the early days of this century. After returning from a trip to Europe, he wrote, if I remember correctly: "Why is it that in Europe, they build a pigsty that looks like a castle and in America, we build a castle that looks like a pigsty!" This certainly applies to the stables at Armadale. It is difficult for visitors who first see the beautiful restaurant and gift shop on the premises to believe that horses and cows were housed there not so long ago.

The Clan Donald Lands centre is a "must" for anyone visiting the Highlands. The half-hour sail from Mallaig on the large car-ferry is the most picturesque way to go, with the hills of Knoydart on the right. The ship docks at Armadale. But the fastest way is to drive over the new bridge to Skye, turn left, and in a few minutes you are at Kinloch Lodge, the award-winning hotel owned and run by Lord and Lady Macdonald. A few miles further on is Sir Iain Noble's *Eilean Iarmain* hotel, where the staff speaks Gaelic, and *Sabhal Mòr Ostaig*, the famous Gaelic college which Sir Iain founded. Then comes the Clan Centre at Armadale.

Ellice McDonald traces his ancestry to Glencoe. The survivors of the Massacre of 1692 fled to neighbouring clans for sanctuary, to the Stewarts of Appin, the Camerons of Lochiel, the MacDonells of Glengarry and Keppoch.

Ellice's great-grandfather went to Glen Garry more than a hundred years later, after the founders of our Canadian Glengarry were long gone. He came as Head Forester to the Rt. Hon. Edward Ellice, MP, owner of what had once been the lands of the MacDonells of Glengarry.

Edward "The Bear" Ellice was a very wealthy man who, as Managing Director of The Hudson's Bay Company, had overseen the amalgamation of that company with The North West Company in the early 1820s. It was through him that young Archibald McDonald, the son of the forester, was given a chance to rise in the world. He was brought into the Hudson's Bay Co.

Archibald McDonald devoted over fifty years of his life to The Bay. He travelled throughout the west, supervising that vast enterprise, and died as the last Chief Factor on active service with the company.

His fearlessness and honesty won him the respect of the native people throughout the west. He lived through some of the most important events in that vast territory during the latter part of the 19th century. He met the great Sioux leader Sitting Bull who had led his people to Canada for asylum after the Battle of the Little Big Horn in 1876. It was due to men like Archibald McDonald and the officers of the North-West Mounted Police, who gained the respect of the natives, that the Sioux lived peacefully for a time in Canada, never so much as stealing a chicken or breaking the law in any way.

Archibald bought a horse from the Sioux that had been captured from the 7th U.S. Cavalry at the Little Big Horn. It lived to a ripe old age and was eventually used by Mrs. McDonald to pull her buggy. As noted in Archibald's memoirs, "When he [the horse] was over in the knees, long in the tooth, spavined and weak in the hind quarters, so that he would sometimes sit down in the shafts" he was taken to a Sunday School picnic. "A brass band began to play, the first he had heard since the Little Big Horn and to the amazement of all, the old grey sprang to life and pranced, danced, and cavorted like a three-year old."

Archibald's son Edward Ellice McDonald, named after his father's benefactor, became a doctor in Montreal in 1901 and then moved to the USA. He had a distinguished career and was the father of Ellice McDonald Jr. who married Rosa Laird of Delaware, where they reside.

For his years of devotion to the Clan Donald Lands Trust and many other philanthropies, Ellice received the CBE, Commander of the Most Excellent Order of the British Empire, from Her Majesty the Queen. His wife Rosa was awarded the same honour a few years later. It is rare enough that this order is given to non-British subjects, and rarer still that it is given to a husband and wife. They are the only couple in North America to have two CBEs.

Ellice and Rosa McDonald are staunch supporters of The Glengarry Highland Society and all Clan Donald Societies the world over. It was largely due to his help originally that the Highland Society is now able to put on the annual Feis-Glengarry and teach the Highland heritage and Gaelic language of our Canadian Glengarry.

The MacLarens

The Clan of Lawrence

The Gaelic name *MacLabhruinn*, "son of Lawrence," is MacLaren or a variation of it in English. It was a small clan, and like so many others, allied itself with larger and more powerful ones. In the case of the MacLarens, those who lived in the North Argyll area of Scotland followed the Stewarts of Appin, while those farther east in the Breadalbane area of Perthshire allied themselves with the Murrays of Atholl. Another branch once held the Inner Hebridean island of Tiree, but those of the clan who came to Glengarry seem to have all originated in Breadalbane.

Although never numerous, the MacLarens were as warlike as any other clan, going into battle at the drop of a hat.

It is east to understand why the other residents of Britain, emerging into the more peaceful and controlled world of the 18th century, would fear these armed people of the Highlands with the hair-triggers and sharp swords. A "gentleman of the clan" up to the middle of that century did not consider himself properly dressed unless he had a sword at his side, one or more pistols in his belt, a dirk at his waist and a small knife, a *sgian dubh*, (pronounced. "skean-doo") in his hose-top or under his arm.

The eventual solution to the disarming of the Highlanders after 1746 led to the government itself taking over the violence, and it was years before the killings and atrocities perpetrated by the British troops on the Highland people ended. But end they eventually did, although a more sinister answer to the "Highland problem" took the place of the overt violence; the Highland Clearances. That was the final solution.

Britain is now one of the most peaceful countries on earth, and tourists can visit without fear the empty Highland glens where a legendary race once lived.

Here in Glengarry the MacLaren name is carried on in the family of Arthur Maclaren, among others. Arthur is descended through his mother Hilda from the famous Sandfield Macdonalds, the leading family in Glengarry in the last century. His Maclaren ancestors came to Glengarry from the Mohawk Valley at the time of the American Revolution.

There were three McLaurin ministers in Glengarry in the early part of the last century, all from the Loch Tay area of Breadalbane in Scotland and all called John.

Rev. John Colin McLaurin of St Andrew's Presbyterian Church in Martintown preached in Gaelic and English. David Anderson of the Bethune-Thompson House has many of his letters and sermons, in both languages. The Rev. John Colin was a great fan of the works of James MacPherson (1736-96), whose controversial translations of the third century poems of Ossian and, in particular, the epic *Fingal*, captured the imagination of the literary world. McLaurin, with some like-minded friends, founded an Ossianic Society.

The Rev. John (Ćraignavie) McLaurin founded the Baptist congregation of Breadalbane here in Lochiel Township in 1816.

The third Rev. John McLaurin was the Presbyterian minister in Kirkhill, also in Lochiel Township, and in L'Orignal. There are plaques to his memory in St Columba's Church, Kirkhill, and in St Andrew's United Church, L'Orignal, which state that he preached in Gaelic and English.

I cannot mention Clan MacLaren without referring to the MacLarens of Buckingham, Quebec. Although not a Glengarry family, they originated in the same area in Scotland as those who came here, and settled on the left bank of the Ottawa. The various MacLaren Companies employed many from Glengarry in the days when men "went to shanty" each year to earn some cash money.

At the Seignory Club in Montebello, the MacLarens of Buckingham held an annual curling bonspiel. There was MacLaren tartan galore, the men in clan blazers, the women in MacLaren skirts.

One year they brought Pipe-Sergeant Andy Ramsay from the famed Black Watch (Royal Highland Regiment) of Montreal to be the personal piper to the aged General MacLaren and to pipe in the head table for the closing dinner. Ramsay was instructed to stick to the old gentleman like glue, piping him into and out of every public room.

During dinner, the General tried to slip quietly away to the men's room. The sergeant, true to his Black Watch training, obeyed his orders to the letter. He leaped up, and before anyone could stop him, piped the red-faced General out of the dining room to the toilet.

Many years ago I was privileged to have been the piper for the MacLaren celebrations at the Seignory Club. At about 2 a.m., long after the

official activities were over, some of the younger members of the group were quietly playing soccer with a tin waste-paper basket in one of the Club's upper corridors while I played a few tunes on the pipes.

Suddenly, Law and Order, in the person of security officer Paddy Coyne appeared. Paddy was a big, fine looking Irishman from the Ottawa Valley, respected and admired by all who knew him for his devotion to duty and his diplomacy.

"Now boys," he said, "there's a little old lady down the hall who has trouble sleeping. Would you please stop kicking that tin thing around and tone down the shouting. And sure now don't we all love the grand music of the pipes, and isn't it the greatest sound in the world, but would you please ask your friend here TO STOP PLAYING THEM!"

Just then, a bedroom door opened and the head of the Buckingham clan, Barnet MacLaren, appeared. "Paddy," he said, obviously trying to pour some oil on the troubled waters, "would you like to come into the suite and have a drink with me?" "Now Mr. Barnet," Paddy replied, "you know well that if I was to accept a drink on duty with you and then the next man and the next and all the other fine gentlemen that would be offering me one I wouldn't be able to perform me duties properly at all do you have any Rye?".

Connections

Bright with names that men remember, loud with names that men forget.
— Swinburne

The connections between Admiral Sir Peter Warren (1704-52), Sir William Johnson of Mohawk Valley fame, and the shadowy and little-known Father John McKenna raise some intriguing questions which bear directly on the early history of British North America, Canada and Glengarry. Some of these questions can be easily answered, others not so easily, and some may never be satisfactorily answered at all.

Who was Sir Peter Warren and how was he connected to Glengarry? The answer is well documented. He was a vice-admiral in the Royal Navy who accumulated great wealth from his share of booty during the war of 1739-48 and invested much of it in the acquisition of land in the Mohawk Valley of the British province of New York.

He placed his nephew Sir William Johnson in charge of his estate there. When he died in 1774, Sir William was the largest landowner in America exceeded only by William Penn of Pennsylvania. And who exactly was Sir William Johnson?

The story of how he brought disbanded Highland soldiers and Palatine Germans to settle on his lands and of how they were forced to leave the Mohawk Valley during the American Revolution and start a new life in Glengarry after he died is well documented. His son Sir John Johnson is remembered because he was the one who led the forced migration of the Highlanders here. Mount Johnson, south of Montreal, was named for him, and he had several imposing residences from St Andrew's East in Quebec, on the left bank of the Ottawa, to Johnson Hall in Williamstown, the place named after his father.

But who really was Sir William Johnson and why did he have such a rapport with the Highland Scots? In most biographies he is referred to as "Anglo-Irish," because he was born in County Meath, Ireland. His mother was Anne Warren, the Admiral's sister, and thanks to that connection he became very rich. But more important to Highland Scots of the 18th century, he evidently claimed to be one of them. The name Johnson was simply the English version of his Gaelic name, *MacIain*, and that name is the patronymic of the chiefs of the MacDonalds of Glencoe.

According to Burke's Peerage, Sir William was descended from the unfortunate victims of the Massacre of Glencoe in 1692. If this genealogy is correct, it would provide a logical answer as to why he was sympathetic to the Highlanders and, in a round-about way, how Glengarry came into being. But there is another connection involving Sir William Johnson and his son Sir John that poses other questions, and some of the answers may never be proved to the satisfaction of professional historians.

This connection involves the Rev. John McKenna. Who was he, how did he become connected with Sir William, and was he, and not the future Big Bishop, the first Roman Catholic chaplain in the British Army since the Reformation? To understand the background to these questions it is necessary to delve a little into history.

After the dissolution of the Catholic church in Britain and Ireland at the Reformation and until the restoration of the hierarchy in 1878, Scotland was officially a "mission" of Rome, served by missionaries. Many of the priests who ministered to the early settlers in Glengarry had been missionaries in Scotland: Fr. Alexander McDonell (Scotus), Fr. Alexander Macdonell (The Big Bishop), Fr. Roderick Macdonell, and, for a short time, Fr. John McKenna.

The Penal Laws made life very difficult for those not professing the state religion, which, in Scotland, see-sawed between the Presbyterian and

Scottish Episcopal churches for a century, until the Presbyterian church became the official church in 1690. There were hardly any Catholics by that time in the Lowlands, but in the Highlands, isolated and conservative, there were large areas that remained staunchly Catholic. It was to minister to these remote parishes that the church sent missionaries.

In the Western Highlands and Islands, these missionaries had to be Gaelic-speaking, and that was how John McKenna came from Ireland to Glen Roy in Lochaber. He soon adapted his Irish Gaelic to the Gaelic idiom of the Highlands and ministered to a parish that extended from Glen Roy through Glengarry to Knoydart on the sea.

In 1773 McKenna came with 425 Highlanders (including "Spanish John" McDonell) on the ship Pearl to New York. Most settled on Sir William Johnson's land in the Mohawk Valley and later came to Canada. As Military Commander of the British Forces in America and because many of the Highland soldiers were Catholics, Sir William reputedly appointed Fr. John Catholic chaplain. If this is historically correct, Fr. John McKenna preceded Fr. Alexander Macdonell as the first Catholic chaplain in the British army since the Reformation by about 20 years. In that case it would be more accurate to refer to the future Big Bishop as "the first Catholic chaplain in the British army in the British Isles since the Reformation."

And where was McKenna from originally? From Meath in Ireland, close to where Sir William had been born. Was there some connection, or was it simply a coincidence?

After Sir William's death, Fr. McKenna came with Sir John Johnson and the exiled Highlanders to Canada and the place they named Glengarry. They soon erected a log church under the direction of McKenna, dedicated to St Andrew. John McKenna, by then a sick man, went home to Ireland and disappeared into history.

A replica of that log chapel now stands in the graveyard across the road from the two later stone churches, the "Blue Chapel" erected with the help of Spanish John, (now the parish hall) and the present church in St Andrew's, just north of Cornwall.

In St Andrew's cemetery rest the bones of Simon Fraser of Fraser River fame, and John Sandfield Macdonald, first premier of Ontario.

Spanish John, a Gentleman of Knoydart

*Never forget that every drop of blood in your veins is that of a Highland
gentleman* — A mother to her young son aboard The Pearl, 1773

Knoydart is in the Western Highlands of Scotland. An area of about 400
sq. miles, it lies between Loch Hourn and Loch Nevis, opposite the Isle of
Skye. No roads traverse it. It can only be reached by climbing some of the
most rugged mountains in Scotland, flying in by helicopter, or hiring a
boat. Two centuries ago it was MacDonell of Glengarry country, although
at one time it was claimed by the MacDonalds of Clanranald.

Knoydart and the MacDonald of Clanranald country adjoining it to the
south were known in olden times, as much for the people who lived there
as for the mountainous terrain, as "the rough bounds." It is certainly high
land, although the term "Highland" refers to the indigenous
Gaelic-speaking people who inhabited the area until recent times. Indeed,
long before the word Highland was coined, most of Scotland was Gaelic
speaking, but the language and the people who spoke it gradually declined
from the 12th century on, and the remnants of the ancient Gaelic race eventually survived only in the more remote Western Highlands and Islands.

The man who became known as "Spanish John" McDonell was born in
1728 at Croulin, sometimes spelled Crowlin, a tack or small land holding at
the entrance to Loch Hourn in Knoydart. His mother-tongue was Gaelic, as
it was for all of his people, although as a "gentleman of the clan" he spoke
English as well. He also spoke French as did many Jacobite Scots supporters of the exiled Stewart dynasty and, as an educated member of the
tacksmen class, had a knowledge of Latin. Later, as his sobriquet denotes,
he acquired Spanish. He was of the house of Scottas, which had provided
several chiefs of the MacDonells of Glengarry.

In an area where there was very little arable land, the hills of Knoydart
were suitable only for the raising of livestock. The problem was that sufficient hay could not be raised for feeding cows during the winter and, as
was the practice in much of the Western Highlands, most of the surplus cattle were sent to the trysts or cattle sales in the south in the autumn.

In some years even oatmeal had to be brought in to provide the basic
food of the people, augmented with fish from the sea, milk and cheese from
their cows and goats, and game from the hills. Whatever sheep they had
were small, half-wild, and could not be easily herded. The huge flocks of
Cheviots and their Lowland shepherds were to come later.

Cattle raids far inland and piracy on the high seas were not unknown to the men of Knoydart. Coll MacDonell of Barisdale, whose tack lay about a dozen miles east of Croulin on Loch Hourn, was notorious in the 18th century as a buccaneer and freebooter. The law of the land, administered from far-off Edinburgh, was largely ignored in the remoter glens of the Highlands. The Stewart king and his heirs, exiled since 1689, were considered by many in Britain to be their rightful rulers and the new government illegitimate.

Although life was hard and cash money seldom seen, the people of Knoydart were imbued with the old Gaelic respect for genealogy. The social position of a gentleman of the clan was not based on wealth, but on ancestry. John McDonell may not have had much in the way of material goods, but he had a noble lineage.

In 1740, at twelve years of age, he was sent by his father to the Scots College in Rome to study for the priesthood. Many years later, in a narrative he wrote of his early life, he described his parting from his father:

> Yet he told me at taking leave, that he did not mean to force my inclination, and that I might act as I thought proper when I should come of years sufficient to form a notion of what would suit my fancy best.

He evidently enjoyed his time studying in Rome and was an apt pupil, but an incident occurred that illustrated his Highland pride. He was falsely accused of a misdemeanour, knocked his accuser down and refused to submit to corporal punishment for his action.

> Without hesitation I avowed my guilt, and I was then told by the Superior that I must undergo the punishment due to my crime. This I refused to comply with, and said such punishments were unworthy of freeborn people.

The Rector of the College was impressed by McDonell's attitude:

> My dear little Johnny, says he, I see you have a great deal of spirit; it must not be broke.

No more was heard of the incident. The Highland attitude to corporal punishment was noted when Highland regiments were formed in the British army. The sadistic application of the lash, a routine punishment in Lowland and English regiments, did not have the desired disciplinary effect on Highlanders. On the few occasions when it was imposed, the victim either deserted or was so demoralized as to be unfit for further military service. The threat of public exposure for cowardice or disobedience was usually enough to ensure the good behaviour of the Highland soldier, to whom bravery and pride were among the highest virtues.

After several years, John McDonell left the Scots College in Rome to become a soldier. He joined the Irish Brigade in the Spanish Army where he found many exiled Jacobite clansmen and Irish McDonells serving as officers. While still in his teens, McDonell saw much action in Italy against the Austrians, was wounded three times, and endured terrible privations.

Obtaining leave from his regiment to join the Jacobite rising of 1745, he was given a fortune in gold to deliver to Prince Charles Edward Stuart but arrived in Scotland too late. The clans had been defeated at Culloden on the very day that he had set sail from France, April 16, 1746.

Spanish John landed at Loch Broom in Wester Ross and set about finding Bonnie Prince Charlie, but was unable to do so. While making his way through the hills to Lochaber, he was robbed of part of the gold by brigands, but was able to deliver the balance to Murray of Broughton who was in hiding with the wounded Cameron of Lochiel at Achnacarry.

There is a persistent rumour that the gold is still buried on Lochiel's land in the Loch Arkaig area.

Spanish John vowed to remain in Scotland until Bonnie Prince Charlie escaped to France. He returned to the fastness of remote Knoydart, where he lived undetected until the following year. He was eventually betrayed by his kinsman Allan MacDonald of Knock in Skye, taken by the notorious Jacobite hunter Capt. Ferguson, accused of treason and put into irons aboard Ferguson's ship.

Transferred to prison in Fort William, Spanish John was released after nine months on insufficient evidence. Returning to Knoydart, he married and lived for many years on his property at Croulin.

At 45 years of age, in 1773, he left with his family and others of his clan on the ship *Pearl* for America. Twenty-five children died on the voyage, and other tribulations awaited them in the New World.

The American War of Independence began a few years after they had settled in the Mohawk Valley of the Province of New York, and the Highland settlers, conservative and royalist to the bone and now reconciled to the Hanoverian dynasty, opposed the rebels. Eventually those who did not sympathize with the revolution, including Spanish John, were forced to leave.

They made their way north through the forest, often with nothing but the clothes on their backs, across the St Lawrence and eventually to crown lands in what is now the most eastern district of Ontario. They called their new settlement Glengarry, in memory of the area in Scotland's Inverness County from which many of them had originated.

Spanish John lived out his long and honourable life among his Highland people in Glengarry, his early Jacobite sympathies abated (at least publicly) by the realization that the Stewart cause was lost forever and that the Georgian dynasty had now proved worthy of allegiance.

In his lifetime, Spanish John had fought and been seriously wounded in the European wars, had seen the bloody aftermath of the defeat of Culloden and the destruction of the ancient clan system of his Gaelic people, escaped death with the Jacobites in the Highland hills, suffered imprisonment for his beliefs, and fought (on the British side) during the American Revolution.

Born into a society that had not changed appreciably for a thousand years, he saw the dawning of the Industrial Age before he died in 1810.

The children of John McDonell and his wife, the daughter of a man killed at Culloden in 1746, followed in the footsteps of their adventuresome father. His son John *le prêtre* chose the life of a fur trader in the North West Company and retired to Pointe Fortune on the Ottawa River. There, at his large and imposing mansion, built in 1818, he entertained in the old Highland style, welcoming the great and the not-so-great to his table.

The house is still there, being lovingly restored by a group which includes both French and English-speaking members and some who trace their ancestry to Spanish John himself. His portrait looks down benignly from the wall in the great dining room.

The Java Man

As I was goin' up the stair / I met a man who wasna there. / He wasna there again today; / I wish to hell he'd go away! — Anon.

There was a time when our primitive ancestors could smell water at a great distance and far underground, as the Bushmen of the Kalahari can still do today. Some say that our remote forebears could converse with animals and birds. The spiritual and the mundane were then as one and the unity of all things was taken for granted. There were members of every tribe who seemed to have perceptions of coming events or of momentous things taking place far away that were taken very seriously and believed without question.

As the nature gods of a simpler day were replaced by the gods of gold, the machine, and science, everything that was not provable was dismissed as nonsense. But in many places, materialism was not completely accepted as the only truth. In some societies, belief in the supernatural survived, in spite of centuries of repression and denial.

Scotland, and in particular that area occupied by the Gaelic-speaking people, was one of those societies.

The story of the Java Man, Donald McLennan, is the quite ordinary and fairly common tale of someone who, for reasons of his own, cuts the ties of home and family and disappears. The extraordinary element in the story lies in the actions of his brother, a child at the time of Donald's disappearance, who, many years later, had what can only be described as a mystical vision of the existence of his brother.

Donald McLennan was seventeen years old when he came with his family from Kintail in the Scottish Highlands to settle in the county of Glengarry in Upper Canada. The lure of high adventure eventually drew him to the fur trade and, at the age of twenty-five, he joined John Jacob Astor's expedition from New York to the mouth of the Columbia River aboard the *Tonquin* in 1810. This ill-fated voyage was to end in tragedy.

The leaders of the expedition were ignorant of the ways of the natives. They did not understand that the natives had no concept of private property. If something caught their fancy in the tepee of another, they took it and no one thought anything of it. Indeed, it was considered a compliment. Sometimes they gave it back (from which the term "Indian-giver" arose) or the previous owner might take something they admired the next time they returned the visit.

While the *Tonquin* was at anchor, some natives came aboard on a friendly visit. A Nez-Perce took a silver goblet and was executed. The terrible result was a raid by the enraged natives and the massacre of all aboard the ship. But Donald McLennan wasn't there. He was up the Columbia River on an exploring expedition. And for the next twenty years, as far as his family knew, he wasn't anywhere.

Donald McLennan was eventually given up for dead, but not by his younger brother Duncan, who seems to have had a strange intuition that things were not as they seemed.

One day Duncan met a Capt. Lovelace, recently retired from the Dutch service. When he learned Duncan's name, the captain looked closely at him. "I knew a man called McLennan," he said. "He was a sugar planter in Java." "What was his first name?" Duncan asked. "I really don't remember," said Lovelace. But from that moment, Duncan knew. He had no proof, no logical explanation, no reason to believe. But just as his forebears could sometimes see visions of the living in far places or the long dead in their own homes, Duncan McLennan knew that his brother was alive and that he would find him.

Even a trip to Montreal was a long and arduous journey in 1844 for a poor farmer from Glengarry, but Duncan made it. And from there he sailed to London, then the centre of world trade, where he was sure to find companies trading with the Dutch East Indies.

At first, the simple country boy, in his homespun suit, was overawed by the sights and sounds of the capital of the British Empire. He couldn't seem to get anywhere with the brusque Londoners. After many days of fruitless enquiries he was about to give up when he found himself at the door of a trading company that advertised the East Indies' connection.

Duncan walked in and told his story to a bored clerk. As he explained his quest in his soft Gaelic accent, a senior member of the firm stopped to listen. "Come into my office," he said. "I want to hear more." When Duncan had finished, he was taken into the office of the head of the firm and repeated his story. "Well, Mr. McLennan," said the senior partner, "if your story is correct, you will soon be able to verify it. Donald McLennan is our agent in Java and will be arriving from Antwerp tonight. Come back tomorrow at eleven and you will meet him. I hope that your hopes will be realized and that he is your brother." They were and he was.

I dreamed a dream the other night / Beyond the Isle of Skye; /
I saw a dead man win a fight / And I think that man was I.
            — Anon

Clan Donald

Fraoch Eilean — (The Heathery Isle) — War Cry of Clan Donald
Creagan an Fhithich — (The Raven's Rock)
— War Cry of the MacDonells of Glengarry
Dia 's Naomh Aindrea — (God and St Andrew)
— War Cry of the MacDonells of Keppoch
Dh'aindeoin co theireadh e — (Gainsay who dare)
— War Cry of the MacDonalds of Clanranald

Why Clan Donald and not Clan MacDonald? The answer is a little complicated. It has to do with the fact that Clan Donald is much more than a single family descended from a common ancestor as is the case in most other clans.

The Donald of the clan name was the grandson of Somerled, the king of the Hebrides, who started it all. Here is how he is described in The Companion to Gaelic Scotland, edited by Derick S. Thomson:

> Gaelic tradition is unanimous in ascribing the creation of the political entity later known as the Lordship of the Isles to Somerled (d. 1164). He was apparently descended from Gofraid, son of Fergus, supporter of Kenneth MacAlpin (d. 858) and leader of the Northern Ui Mac Uais settled in the Hebrides at least as early as the seventh century. Somerled began his successful offensive against Norse overlordship in Argyll, and he was probably leader of a contingent from there in the army of David I that invaded England in 1138. He supported an unsuccessful rebellion by his nephews, the sons of Malcolm Mac Heth, immediately following the accession of Malcolm IV in 1153 as a minor and contrary to the rules of tanistry. He then turned to the recovery of the Hebrides ruled by the king of Man under Norse suzerainty which he probably regarded as his ancestral homeland. In 1156 and again in 1158 he defeated the king of Man, who fled to Norway. From his Gaelic title, *Ri Innse Gall* (King of the Hebrides), borne also by his successors, derives the Latin *Dominus Insularum* (Lord of the Isles), first recorded in 1354. Somerled was killed near Renfrew in 1164, having led another rebellion against Malcolm IV.

The Lordship of the Isles included parts of the mainland of Scotland and of the north-east of Ireland and all the islands from the Isle of Man in the Irish Sea to the Butt of Lewis, the most northern spot in the Hebrides. The Lords of the Isles ruled their territory as a separate kingdom from Scotland for hundreds of years.

Only those directly descended from Somerled's grandson Donald are really MacDonalds by blood. A great many of those calling themselves MacDonald (or any of the many variations of the name) are those whose ancestors adopted the name because it was expedient to do so. This was common practice in the days of clan feuds when the wrong name could get you into big trouble.

All those identifying with Clan Donald were known in Gaelic as *MacDhomhnuill* or as *Domhnullach* (of Donald, or belonging to Clan Donald). The same practice of identifying with a first name was followed centuries later by the supporters of the Stewart king James VII, and were known as Jacobites after the Latin for James, *Jacobus*. In Ireland, the followers of the powerful Fitzgeralds (*fils*, son) were known as the Geraldines, although few were actually descended from the original Gerald.

When speaking Gaelic, members of Clan Donald (unless they are directly descended from the original Donald, as are all the chiefs of the various branches of the clan) simply refer to themselves a *Domhnullach*. No other clan has this distinction. There is no equivalent word in English, unlike the Fitzgerald *Geraldines*. In English (and who uses the original Gaelic of their names anymore?) the name is MacDonald or whatever version of the name is used in your particular family.

The Clan Donald Society of Glengarry-Stormont was revived a few years ago under the aegis of Duncan (darby) MacDonald. It is only natural that the clan has an active group in this area. I don't believe that there is any place in Scotland that has such a heavy concentration of that clan as in this part of the world. In the First War, there were more MacDonalds (and all the variations of the name) in the Canadian army than Smiths.

You don't have to bear the actual name to belong to Clan Donald. As well as dozens of family names or "septs," from Alexander to Whannell, there are clan names such as the MacAlisters of Loup, closely connected with the leadership of Clan Donald for hundreds of years.

How the MacAlisters of Loup could have been so closely associated with the MacDonells of Glengarry has always puzzled me. Loup, from the Gaelic *lub*, which means a bend in a river, is in the parish of Kilfinnan, far to the south of the Scottish Glengarry in the area known as Kerry in Argyll.

The MacAlisters inhabited that area ever since Clan Donald ruled the Kingdom of the Isles in the 12th century. Eventually the Campbells expanded throughout Argyll and the MacAlisters found themselves isolated from their Glengarry clanspeople.

It is interesting that the MacAlisters once lived in the parish of Kilfinnan, which means the Church of St Finnan. All branches of Clan Donald seemed very fond of the memory of that obscure saint of the early Celtic Church. There are churches named after him at Glenfinnan in MacDonald of Clanranald country, at Invergarry in MacDonell of Glengarry territory and of course in Alexandria, the County Seat of our Canadian Glengarry.

The Gentle Giant of Glentarry

The champion of the heavy events

When he was seventeen he leaped over three horses standing side by side. He could run faster and throw the hammer farther than anyone in Glengarry. Eventually, no one in Canada or the States could beat him at the hammer-throw. Scotland's greatest heavy-events champion, Donald Dinnie, refused to compete against him. He was proclaimed world champion several times. Because of his enormous strength and quiet nature, the sportswriters of the day dubbed him "The Gentle Giant of Glengarry." He was Roderick R. "Big Rory" McLennan, the greatest athlete that Glengarry ever produced.

Big Rory's ancestors came from Kintail, a remote area of the Scottish Highlands opposite the Isle of Skye. The people of Kintail, Macraes, MacKenzies and MacLennans and their Chisholm neighbours to the north were noted for their size and strength. The McLennans of Glen Donald, Charlottenburgh Township, Glengarry County, were no exception. Rory and his brothers were all big and immensely strong, but coupled with that strength was an agility that is rare in big men. They could run as well as they could put the shot or throw the hammer.

Big Rory's father was a veteran of the Rebellion of 1837, serving in the Glengarry Militia. Although the rising in Upper Canada was led by a Scot whose mother-tongue was Gaelic, William Lyon MacKenzie, there was little sympathy for him in Glengarry and the area remained loyal.

Big Rory's mother was descended from the McDonalds of Munial in Knoydart and was the niece of Big Finnan the Buffalo, the man who had wrestled an enraged bull buffalo to a standstill on the Canadian prairie in 1827. Big Rory inherited his remarkable strength from both sides of the family.

Feats of strength and fame in the heavy events at Caledonian Games were only part of Big Rory's life. He built rail lines through some of the most difficult terrain in Canada. He founded a bank and three newspapers.

After several defeats, he was elected to the Ontario Legislature in 1892. He was a contractor, banker, and a soldier as well.

He suffered some criticism for some of his activities as a builder of rail lines. It was the age of "railroad barons" and even Canada's first prime minister was involved in a railway scandal.

But no one ever questioned Big Rory's athletic prowess. Unfortunately, all the fame and fortune in the world could not make up for the one great tragedy of his life. In 1877, at the age of 35, he gave an exhibition throw of the hammer at the Queen's Anniversary festivities in Cornwall, Ontario. The hammer struck and killed a young woman who had wandered onto the field. Rory never threw the hammer again.

Big Rory died in 1907, and was buried in the graveyard of St.Andrew's Presbyterian Church in Williamstown.

The MacSweyns

Courage is the thing. All goes if courage goes — J. M. Barrie

The recent death of Ralph MacSweyn, one of the strongest men who ever lived in Glengarry, started me thinking about the origins of this clan.

Sweyn is a Norse name, spelled in many different ways, but the Scottish Gaelic spelling is usually *Suain*. The name came to Scotland with the Vikings, the Norsemen who raided and eventually ruled the Western Isles and vast areas of the Scottish mainland.

Many clans trace their beginnings to this turbulent era a thousand years ago and the Norse connection remains in their names, such as MacLeod, "Son of Leod" and MacAulay, "Son of Olaf." The Gaelic for the Scandinavian Peninsula is *Lochlann*, the "Land of Lochs," because of the numerous sea-lochs or fjords which indent the coastline there, so "MacLachlan" means "Son of the Norseman."

There are many variations of Highland names, of course, as there are of all family names, and in Gaelic "mac," meaning "son," is often abbreviated to "mc" or even simply "m." (There is no truth, by the way, in the notion that "Mc" is Irish and/or Catholic and "Mac" Scottish and/or Protestant). The names themselves were spelled phonetically before Gaelic spelling was standardized in the 18th century and even today many names are spelled differently by members of the same clan or family.

Even if a name like MacMillan is now written about six different ways, it is an improvement on the way it was spelled in old documents, where it appears in over 150 variations. Standard English evolved at about the same time, writers before the end of the 18th century not being overly concerned about spelling. Shakespeare spelled his name several different ways as is shown in examples of his signature.

The dominance of Norway in the west and north of Scotland was challenged in the 12th century under the leadership of Somerled, the Gaelic-Norse progenitor of the mighty Clan Donald. As a descendant of the ancient aristocracy of Dalriada he became *Regulus Insularum*, the King of the Isles, a term not loved by British monarchists of a later day, who preferred, and still prefer, the more innocuous term Lord of the Isles.

Somerled and his successors ruled a sea-kingdom from the Isle of Man through Antrim in Ulster, including all of the Hebrides. The MacSweyns, though never a large clan, were important supporters of the King of the Isles.

The name MacSweyn has one variation that is particularly interesting here in Glengarry — MacQueen. How this came about is difficult for a non-Gaelic speaker to understand, but it is really quite simple. Most Gaelic names are now known only in their English versions and as there is no w, y, or q in the Gaelic alphabet, we must go to the Gaelic spelling first. MacSweyn is *MacSuain* in Gaelic, and in some dialects the genitive "of" as in "Son of Suain," is formed by dropping the first letter of the word following, so MacSuain becomes what sounds like MacWain. The hard "c" of "Mac" is carried over to the name and to emphasize this in English, somewhere along the line a "Q" was introduced, producing MacQueen. Another variation is Sween, as in Castle Sween, the ancient stronghold of the clan in Kintyre. The name Sweeney originates there.

The untimely death of Ralph MacSweyn of Laggan occurred in 1995. There are many tales about his feats of strength here in Glengarry. Darrel MacLeod tells of the time, some twenty years ago, when the R.D. MacLeod farmhouse in Laggan was set on fire. The neighbours rushed in to help save some of the furniture. There was a large freezer chest full of food in the cellar which several men struggled to get out through the narrow door. It became wedged in, and all their struggles were in vain. Luckily Ralph

MacSweyn was on the inside. "Get out of the way," he shouted to the straining men. He lifted the end of the chest and with a mighty shove, pushed it out the door.

Generations of MacSweyns here in Glengarry were noted for their Gaelic singing as well as their athletic abilities. At *Feis-Glengarry '95*, The Glengarry Gaelic Choir dedicated a song to Ralph MacSweyn's memory. It was about bravery and courage.

The MacDonalds of Keppoch

Will the real chief please stand up?

Although this clan was not nearly as numerous or as powerful as their kinsfolk, the MacDonells of Glengarry or the MacDonalds of Clanranald, they gave a good account of themselves for centuries in the Highlands of Scotland. They occupied an area in Lochaber that included Glen Roy and Glen Spean, and held it "by the sword" against all comers, including the MacIntoshes who at one time claimed it.

In the years after the defeat of the Jacobites at Culloden in 1746 their land was forfeited to the Crown and, as was the case with so many others, most MacDonalds (or MacDonells, as they sometimes spelled their name) of Keppoch were forced to leave their ancestral homes.

Following is an article that appeared in The Oban Times, Scotland, of September 21, 1935, sent to me years ago by my friend Rory MacDonald of Glen Spean.

> John de Lotbiniere MacDonald, 22nd Chief of the MacDonalds of Keppoch, died on Aug. 14 in the Montreal General Hospital in his 78th year. A member of an old Scottish Canadian family, Mr. MacDonald was widely known.
>
> Mr. MacDonald was the eldest son of the late A.E. de Bellefueille MacDonald and of Louise Harwood de Lotbiniere and grandson of the late John MacDonald of Garth, last surviving Partner of the old North West Company. He was also a grandnephew of the late Hon. William MacGillivray, Chief Partner of the Company, and of Lieut.-General Sir Archibald Campbell of Ava, Governor of New

Brunswick in 1834. The late Col. A.C. de Lotbiniere Harwood, Seigneur of Vaudreuil, the late Rt. Hon. Sir Elzear Taschereau, Chief Justice of Canada and the late Sir Henry Joly de Lotbiniere were his uncles.

He was a resident of Alexandria in the old Scottish settlement of Glengarry. Of splendid physique, his sympathetic disposition, his generosity, and his irrepressible sense of humour, endeared him to the population of Glengarry.

The MacDonalds of Keppoch were a warlike branch of Clan Donald. They were noted for their loyalty to the house of Stewart, to which they were closely allied, and stood by Bonnie Prince Charlie to the last. The House of Keppoch descends from Alistair Carrach of the Isles, Lord of Lochaber, and of Princess Margaret, daughter of Robert II, King of Scotland, and granddaughter of Robert the Bruce.

In 1640 Angus of Keppoch, 12th Chief, was killed in a fight with the Campbells of Breadalbane at a place called Stronlachan, leaving minor children. His uncle, Donald *Glass* MacDonald, became their tutor, but they were deprived of their rights to the Keppoch succession and became MacDonalds of Achnacoichean. In 1889 the younger branch, which had continued the line as Chiefs of Keppoch, became extinct, and the Chieftainship, after 300 years, returned to the Achnacoicheans, the eldest branch of the Keppochs, of which the late Mr. MacDonald was the representative.

On the maternal side, Mr. MacDonald was allied with the de Lotbinieres, de Lerys, the Vaudreuils, Le Gardeurs and St Ours, leading families of the old Canadian noblesse. Mr. MacDonald is survived by two brothers, Charles de B. MacDonald, A. de Lery MacDonald, and a sister, Miss de Bellefeuille, all of Rigaud. The funeral service was held in the Parish Church of Rigaud.

The statements in The Oban Times about Mr. MacDonald's Canadian connections are correct, but there are errors in his Scottish genealogy and his claim to the chiefship of the MacDonalds of Keppoch was never validated or accepted. Rory MacDonald himself has been involved in the search for the legitimate chief of his clan for many years.

The Auld Alliance between Scotland and France, going back six hundred years, is echoed in Canada by this illustrious family. Scottish troops fought for Joan of Arc in the 15th century and expatriate Scots soldiers in *la garde écossaise* were the bodyguards of the French monarchy for hundreds of years. The story of the Scots in the French service is the theme of Sir Walter Scott's novel *Quentin Durward.*

Highland paths have many twists and turnings, joining and branching off along the roads of history as in the case of the MacDonalds of Keppoch and their kin, who contributed so much to the building of Canada.

The first Scots who came to this land in the service of France before 1759, such as Ramezay and the Chevalier de Johnstone, blazed the trail that later Scottish settlers followed. Deprived of their native glens, they were in the vanguard of the makers of this country. In a sense, much of early Canada could be termed New Scotland.

Big Finnan the Buffalo

But when the pride of their strength arose, they shook the hill with their heels; rocks tumble from their places on high; the green-headed bushes are overturned. Ossian's Fingal.

The bull buffalo charged, throwing Finnan in the air and tearing open his thigh from knee to waist. He struggled, half-fainting, to his feet. The buffalo charged again. Finnan threw himself at the huge head, grasping the bull by the nostrils with one hand and by one lethal horn with the other. There was a muffled snap and Finnan realized that his wrist had been dislocated. He could no longer hold onto the horn. His hand slipped down to the shock of hair on the forehead of the buffalo. He gave a great shout of rage and man and beast crashed to the ground.

Over the next three hours they wrestled, alternating between frantic lunges and exhaustion. The witnesses to this titanic battle could not get close enough to shoot the animal without endangering the man. Finally, when night began to fall, the two combatants collapsed, seemingly lifeless. While rushing in to save Finnan, or what was left of him, one of the rescuers' guns accidentally discharged, rousing the buffalo, and it lumbered off. The ground was torn and bloodied over a large area, but Finnan was still alive.

David Douglas, the Scots botanist who was one of the party of explorers accompanying Finnan, bound his wounds and discovered that as well as the obvious injuries, he had suffered two broken ribs and was horribly bruised over most of his body. But within a few days Big Finnan the Buffalo, as he was to be known for the rest of his life, regained his strength and resumed his place as guide of the expedition. His bungled attempt to obtain fresh meat for his party of explorers had guaranteed his place in Canadian history.

The year was 1827, on the Western Plains of Canada near the Saskatchewan River. One of the other witnesses present on that occasion was David Thompson, the renowned cartographer. But who was Big Finnan?

Finnan McDonald was originally an employee of the North West Company, the Montreal-based fur trading empire that extended from Quebec to the Pacific. When the "Canadian Company" as it was familiarly known, was amalgamated with the "English Company," the Hudson's Bay Company, in 1821, Finnan and many other Nor'Westers became part of that powerful enterprise which had flourished since 1670.

Unlike "The Bay" which recruited many Lowland Scots from the Orkney Islands to manage its trading posts, the Nor'Westers were mostly Gaelic - speaking Highland Scots who had left their native land in the years after the Jacobite Rising of 1745 and the defeat of Culloden. The brutal reprisals visited on the Highland people in the years following that debacle had resulted in the destruction of the clan system and had made emigration the only possibility for many.

The first organized Highland settlements in British North America were in the Carolinas, but after the defeat of the French in 1759, Canada and the fur trade drew men like Alexander McKenzie, Simon Fraser, and Simon McTavish, and in 1779 the North West Company was established.

Finnan McDonald was born in 1772 in Knoydart, a remote area of the Scottish Highlands to the west of Glen Garry, facing the Isle of Skye. His father, Angus Bàn of Muineal, left Scotland forever with his family when Finnan was a young boy. They settled in the new Glengarry, Upper Canada (now the Province of Ontario).

In 1804 Finnan entered the service of the North West Company. His lack of formal education barred him from becoming a partner in the company, but he had other attributes. His large size and strength soon made him a legend.

The Irish journalist Ross Cox wrote of him in 1813, fourteen years before his wrestling match with the buffalo:

> He spoke Gaelic, English, French, and several Indian dialects. Standing six feet four, his uncut flaming red hair and beard gave him a wild appearance. Gentle as a lamb, he had the courage of a lion. He was particularly affectionate to men of small size and would stand their bantering. However, let one of his own size take

advantage of his good nature and his lowering look would warn of an approaching eruption.

Finnan's mother was a Macrae from Kintail, a clan famed for strength and endurance. One of Finnan's brothers, John *le borgne* (one-eyed in the French used by the Nor'Westers as often as English) led an adventuresome life in the North West Co. and later in the Hudson's Bay Co. He assisted Sir John Franklin in his ill-starred attempts to discover the Northwest Passage. Although he did not accompany Franklin on the trip that ended with the loss of the entire expedition, Lady Franklin thought so much of John Mc-Donald's support of her husband that she had a memorial raised to him after his death in Newmarket, Ontario.

Finnan himself explored vast areas of the West and was the first white man to build a dwelling in the Oregon Territory.

Big Finnan the Buffalo retired to Glengarry County, Ontario, as did many Nor'Westers. He died in 1851 and is buried with his native wife, the daughter of a Plains chief, in the graveyard of the historic Catholic church of St Raphael's, where he rests with six generations of his Highland people. Until recently, no stone marked his grave.

Finnan "The Buffalo" McDonald wrestling with the bull buffalo -
from the sketch by Donald MacDonald, courtesy of
Dr. Hugh P. MacMillan and The Glengarry Historical Society.

APPENDIX

Nicknames, patronymics and pedigrees in Glengarry.

A nickname is described in The Oxford Paperback Dictionary as "a name given humorously to a person instead of or as well as his or her real name," a patronymic as "a person's name taken from the name of the father or a male ancestor" and pedigree as "a line of ancestors, especially a distinguished one."

In a Highland community there are often so many with similar names that further identification is necessary to avoid confusion. In Glengarry, before the government gave us all numbers, banks and post offices kept lists of nicknames, and it is from one of those lists that the following have been culled. Some of these names applied to one person only, others to the family for generations.

Another form of identification (as seen, for instance, in the stained glass windows in St Finnan's Cathedral, Alexandria) consisted of the location of the original farm or land grant: *Lot #, concession # and township.*

The ability to name one's ancestors back many generations is natural to the Highland people and some, even today, can reel off their pedigrees with ease, such as Angus Rory MacDonald of St Raphael's, *Angus Rory Angus Ranald Rory Angus.* In the Gaelic tradition, each name would be preceded by *mac*, which becomes *mhic* (vik) in the genitive case and *nic* (neek) in the feminine. So Angus Rory's *sloinneadh* (sloin-uh) would be: *Aonghas mac Ruairidh mhic Aonghais mhic Raonuill mhic Ruairidh mhic Aonghais,* representing five generations.

Originally, almost all of the hundreds of nicknames in Glengarry would have been in Gaelic, but as it was a spoken, not a written language to most, some strange spellings evolved. As the Gaelic meaning of a name was gradually forgotten, the misspelling could be misunderstood. *Hughie the Crock,* for instance, may be interpreted several ways in English, but "crock" is simply the pronunciation of the Gaelic *cnoc*, a hill, so the original Crock probably lived on a hill or rise.

My wife Anne, daughter Sine and I, with the help of many in the area, have tried to interpret the Gaelic-sounding nicknames on the following list, but unless a meaning is verified, can only suggest possibilities. If there are several meanings for the same Gaelic word, we have tried to select the most obvious. A word that sounds or looks obscene or peculiar in the English version may not actually be so, the Gaelic original having a completely different meaning. Sometimes a seemingly innocuous English word may have a shocking Gaelic origin.

The list has been divided according to family names. Please note that *Mac* or *Mc* is interchangeable, the spelling often changing from generation to generation or even within the same family and is not an infallible method of identification. In the list as we were given it, *Mac* is almost always used throughout and many *MacDonalds* should probably be *MacDonells*. It should be noted that Alex, in the Scottish tradition, is pronounced Alec.

The more prevalent a family name, the more nicknames were necessary. The MacDonalds (whatever the spelling), formed such a large proportion of the population that they naturally had the most nicknames by far. It is obvious that if a family name was rare in the community there would be little need of a distinctive appellation.

Some of these names may date from the earliest days in Glengarry, some may be more modern and some persons may have more than one nickname. It should also be noted that Donald and Daniel are the same in Gaelic, *Domhnall*. Although most patronymics refer to the male line, a few include women, such as the Angus Katie MacDonalds.

There are many nicknames on this list that cannot be interpreted.

Allan MacDonald ... Allan the Butcher
Allan MacDonald ... Allan the Bruch (possibly *bruach* - surly)
Allan MacDonald ... Allan the Wheelwright
Allan MacDonald ... Allan Little Ranald
Allan MacDonald ... Allan the Wolf
Allan J. MacDonald ... Pobs
Allan MacDonald ... Allan the Cleaver (poss. from *cladhaire*,
     which can mean either hero, coward, grave-digger or rogue!)
Allan MacDonald ... Allan the Bruch (Poss. bruchach —
     freckled-face)
Alex MacDonald ... Slippery Alex
Alex MacDonald ... Alex the Saddler
Alex MacDonald ... Alex at Rory's
Alex MacDonald ... Sandy the Banker
Alex MacDonald ... Big Alex the Calf
Alex MacDonald ... Blind Alex

Alex MacDonald ... Alex the Elder

Alex MacDonald ... Alex Lemon (poss. *leòmag* - conceited

Alex MacDonald ... Alex Slave (poss. *sliabh* — side of the hill)

Alex MacDonald ... Brother Paul

Angus MacDonald ... Angus the Mason

Angus MacDonald ... Little Angus the Keg (poss. *caig* — a tease)

Angus MacDonald ...Angus Katie

Angus MacDonald ... Angus Bitters

Angus MacDonald ... Angus Nuck (poss. *nuagach* — sunken-eyed)

Angus MacDonald ... Angus the Widow Hughie Rory Tailor

Angus R. MacDonald ... Tuffany No. 2

Angus Roy MacDonald ... Gilly Rugh (*Gille Ruadh* - the Red-haired
    Boy)

Angus MacDonald ... Angus Chuck

Angus MacDonald ... Angus the Chunck

Angus A. MacDonell ... Angie Alex Big Duncan

Archie MacDonald ... Archie Moutarst (from *Mùideart*, Moidart, a
    district in Scotland)

Archie MacDonald ... Archie and a half

Archie MacDonald ... Rotten Archie (could be from *Rotan*, red-faced)

Archie MacDonald ... Archie the Cramish (poss. *crambach* —
    quarrelsome)

Archie John MacDonald ... Archie John Mackinaw

Archie MacDonald ... Katie Veck (*Bheag* - fem. nominative for little)

Catherine MacDonald ... Katie Aunty

Charles MacDonald ... Charlie Big Ranald Dan MacDonald
        ... Schenectady (poss. brought from the Mohawk Valley
    of New York)

Christopher MacDonald ... Gillie Alex Archie (*Gille*, short for Gaelic
Gille-Chriosd, Christopher)

Christopher MacDonald ... Gillie Ranald Rory ... (see above)

Dan MacDonald ... Danny Marjorie

Dan MacDonald ... Dan Agent

Dan Angus MacDonald ... Black Angus

Dan MacDonald ... Cotillion

Dan MacDonald ... Dan Brown

Dan R. Macdonald ... Danny Rory Oon (*Uan* - lamb)

Dan MacDonald ... Darby*

Dan MacDonald ... Danny Mulligan (from a lumber camp boss of
        the same name or from *Murlaggan*, Glen Roy, Scotland)

Dan D. MacDonald ... Danny Donald Big Jim

Donald MacDonald ... High Donald

Donald MacDonald ... Big Donald the Blacksmith

Donald MacDonald ... Donald Boots

Donald MacDonald ... Donald the Keg (poss. *caig* — a tease)

Donald MacDonald ... Donald the Potash

Donald MacDonald ... Donald in the Grove

Donald MacDonald ... Donald Big John the Post

Donald MacDonald ... Donald Satan (poss. a Gaelic meaning undiscovered)

Duncan MacDonald ... Snatch Block (poss. *sneachd ploc* — snowball)

Duncan MacDonald ... Duncan the Owl

Duncan MacDonald ... Dakota Dunc

Duncan MacDonald ... Dunkie Dotion (?)

Duncan MacDonald ... Dunkie the Bush

Duncan MacDonald ... Dunkie the Rogue

Duncan MacDonald ... Duncan the Singer

Duncan MacDonald ... Duncan Spoggie, Black Hand(?) (*Spògach* is clumsy-footed)

Duncan MacDonald ... Duncan Austin

George MacDonald ... Zick (possibly *seig* — bellyfull)

George MacDonald ... George Black Sandy

George MacDonald ... George of Atholl

Hugh MacDonald ... Hughie the Farmer

Hugh MacDonald ... Hughie Stinker

Hugh MacDonald ... Hughie the Crock (*cnoc* - hill, pro. "crok")

Hugh P. MacDonald ... Hughie the Piper

Kate MacDonald ... Kate Noah (?)

John A. Macdonell ... Jack Greenfield

James MacDonald ... Jimmy the Queen   (Gaelic origin unknown)

John Angus MacDonald ... Johnny Kintail (Kintail is north of the Scottish Glengarry)

John MacDonald ... The Square

John MacDonald ... Johnny the Sawmill

John MacDonald ....Johnny Alex the Cook

John MacDonald ... John Bunyon (poss. *bunain* — stubble)

John MacDonald ... Johnny Stoppan (*stòpan* — drop of whisky)

John MacDonald ... Johnny John the Captain

John MacDonald ... Johnny the Blackbird

John MacDonald ... Johnny Lot (poss. *lot* — to wound or stab, or *loth*, beard)

John MacDonald ... Johnnie the Nun

John MacDonald ... Johnny the Oats

John MacDonald ... Big John the Flag

John MacDonald ... Caesar (poss. from *ceas* — kiss)

John MacDonald ... The Officer

John A. MacDonald ... Johnny Alex Peter John Donald

John Duncan MacDonald ... The Detective

John Kenneth MacDonald ... Garden Field

John MacDonald ...Cain Mohr (*ceann mor* — big head)

John R. MacDonald ... Johnny Egg Nog (poss. connected with
    the Isle of Eigg & the Eigg Road here in Glengarry).

John R. MacDonald ... Johnny Ranald Clavehurst
      (poss. from an attachment to Graham of Claverhouse, "Bonnie
Dundee.")

John R. MacDonald ... Johnny Hank

John MacDonald ... Stuttering John

John MacDonald ... Marcelly (from Marcellus?)

John MacDonald ... Three Cups of Tea

John MacDonald ... Black John the Priest

John MacDonald ... Johnny Two Thumbs

John MacDonald ... Johnny the Widow at the Corner

John MacDonald ... John the Pedlar

Mrs. John MacDonald ... Old Woman Knoidart

Joseph MacDonald ... Blue Room Joe

Katie MacDonald ... Ice Cream Katie

Laughlin MacDonald ... Lachlin Owen Og (*òg* - young)

Margaret MacDonald ... Maggie Rory Down (*Donn* - Brown-haired)

Mrs. Mary MacDonald ... Big Mary, Mary Vorre (*Mairi Mhor*)

Mrs. Mary MacDonald ... Little Mary, Mary Vech (*Mairi Bheag*)

Mary MacDonald ... Mary the Valley

Nancy MacDonald ... Cracked Nancy (poss. *cràcach* —
    tousled-haired)

Neil MacDonald ... Allan Balla Vhean (*Baile - Bheagan* - Little Town)

Peter MacDonald ... Peter Hughie Allan

Peter MacDonald ... Peter Angus Dougall

Ranald MacDonald ... Long Ranald

Ranald MacDonald ... Ranald the Rapids

Ranald MacDonald ... Lame Ranald the Cruppuck (*crùbach* — lame)

Ronald MacDonald ... Black Ronald

Rory MacDonald ... Kith-Me-Betsy

Rory MacDonald ... Rory Little Widow

Rory MacDonald ... Rory the Alligator

Rory MacDonald ... Rory Back of the Swamp

Rory MacDonald ... Rory the Brown House

Sandy MacDonald ... Long Nose Sandy

Sandy MacDonald ... Sandy McGehan Have an Onion (root word poss.
    abhainn, river)

Sandy MacDonald ... Sandy the Ocean (prob. *Ossian*, the Gaelic poet)

Sandy MacDonald ... Sandy Swift

Sandy MacDonald ... Lochaber

Sandy MacDonald ... Sandy John Allan

Thomas MacDonald ... Thomas Con

William MacDonald ... Willie Buffalo

William MacDonald ... Thundering Bill

John Macdonell ... Darby* (see footnote)

John Cameron ... Cariboo

John Cameron ... Camarat John

Donald Campbell ... Cas-Beech (Gaelic *Cas*, foot, and Eng.
    Beech, the wood from which his wooden leg was made)

Donald Campbell ... Donald Blue (gorm is blue; could
      be a translation or have other meaning.
      Blue is a family name as well)

Angus Chisholm ... Row Back Chisholm (*robach*, shaggy and filthy)

Donald Kennedy ... Donald Fricken (poss. from *freac*, bent or bending)

Hugh Kennedy ... Sheepskin Kennedy

John Kennedy ... Johnny Sport

John Kennedy ... John Isabel

William Kennedy ... Hairy William, Uilleam Ròmach

Willie MacArthur ... Con Darby*

Duncan MacCormick ... Proud Duncan

John MacCrimmon ... John Bull (could be the obvious, or from
    boile, furious)

Angus MacDougall ... Big Angus the Clap (*clab*, thick-lipped
    or garrulous)

John MacDougald ... Johnny Rory the Fiddler

John MacDougall ... Johnny Cement

John MacDougall ... Sweaty John

Ranald MacDougall ... Ranald Donald Archie

Ranald MacDougall ... Krongers MacDougall (from Gaelic pro.
    of Knoydart, *Cnoideart*)

Dan MacGillivray ... Roaring Dan

Donald McGillis ... Day Pawle (meaning obscure)

John MacGillis ... The Gilla Pooer (poss. *Gille bodhar*, deaf person)

Donald MacGillis ... Donald the Pope

Alex McIntosh ... Waterloo

Dan McIntosh ... Windsor Dan

Alex MacKinnon ... Pretty Alex

Archie MacKinnon ... Archie Greasac (poss. From
    griosach, imprecating or swearing)

Archie MacKinnon ... Archie Cah Up (?)

Ranald MacKinnon ... The Deer

Dan Allan Archie MacLeod ... Doctor

Norman MacLeod ... One-eyed Norman

Jane MacLeod ... Lightning Jane

Angus MacLennan ... Angus the Rooster

Dan MacLennan ... Buffalo Dan

John MacLennan ... Johnny the Duke

Ranald MacLellan ... Gordie Scratch Block (?)

Archie J. MacMillan ... Red Archie

Allan MacMillan ... Allan Red Vest

Dr. MacMillan ... The Senator

Duncan MacMillan ... Darachey (poss. from *darach*, oak —
    the badge of the Camerons)

Duncan MacMillan ... The Dutchwoman

Donald MacMillan ... Donald the Deacon

Duncan MacMillan ... Dunkie Fisk (poss. From
    Fiske's Corner, Kenyon Twp.)

Hugh MacMillan ... Corribooie (*Coire*, a gully and *buidhe*,
    golden, poss. a placename in Scotland)

John MacMillan ... John Bnidge (poss. misprint from
    buidhe, see above)

John MacMillan ... Johnny Ban Bog (*bàn*, fair-haired, boc, timid)

James MacNaughton ... Jimmy Pork

Angus MacNaughton ... Croppie

Alex MacPhee ... Sandy Moigans (*mùigean*, surly)

Angus MacPhee ... Sefeckie (poss. from *seafaid*, a heifer)

Angus MacPhee ... Angus the Drover

Duncan MacPhee ... Duncan Donald Angus at the Bridge

Allan MacRae ... Allan the Square

Christopher MacRae ... (*brocair*, a fox-hunter)

Duncan MacRae ... Buckeye

*As an example of how difficult it is to interpret some nicknames, several Glengarry families carry the "Darby" nickname. Duncan (Darby) MacDonald of Brockville, Ont., wrote me the following on Aug. 29, 1998. "The family nickname Darby boils down to three possibilities as I have determined over the years." Duncan goes on to list them:

1) Darby, from "Darby and Joan," the 18th century conventional example of a happily-married old couple. [It is highly unlikely that this origin would have been familiar to Gaelic-speaking Highland people].

2) From the English word for a plasterer's tool. [and several other meanings].

3) From town called Darby (Derby?) in Delaware or Pennsylvania where the emigrant ship *Cochrane* was reputedly forced to spend the winter of 1786-87.

David Anderson of Williamstown offers the additional possibility that the name originated with Darby Bergin, surgeon-general of militia circa 1860 and a leading citizen of Cornwall, Ontario.

[There is also a Derby St. in Alexandria. "Darby" is the southern English pronunciation.]

ᐯy Book Lisτ

A man will turn over half a library to make one book — Samuel Johnson

These are some of the publications from my library which I use in the preparation of my Highland Paths stories. As I am not an academic, it is a rather eclectic and personal list. Many publications on it are out of print or otherwise not easily available. For those readers who may wish to learn more about the story of the Highland Scots, I have marked with an * those books which are currently available through bookshops.

My favourites are: Anything by James Hunter or John Prebble and, of course, Marianne McLean's definitive work on Glengarry.

Here in Glengarry, a good selection is available at Danskin's Scottish Shop, Main St, Maxville, Ont. KOC 1TO, (613) 527-2037 and the Glengarry Book Store, 124 Main St S, Alexandria, Ont. KOC 1EO, (613) 525-1313. For rare and out-of-print Scottish and Gaelic books, Donald MacCormick, Antiquarian Bookseller, 19 Braid Crescent or 140 Comiston Road, Edinburgh, Scotland, EH1O 6AX, phone 0131 447 2889 or Fax 0131 447 9496, is tops.

A note of warning: Many publications on the Highland Scots before the middle of this century are biased and unreliable. Antiquity does not guarantee accuracy.

*Bain, Robert. *The Clans and Tartans of Scotland.* **(many editions).**

Belden's Illustrated Historical Atlas of Stormont, Dundas and Glengarry Counties. Ontario 1879; reprinted Mika 1972.

Black, George F. *The Surnames of Scotland.* New York, 1946.

Boswell, James. *Journal of a Tour to the Hebrides.* (many editions)

Buchanan, Donald. *Reflections of the Isle of Barra.* London, 1942.

Bumsted, J. M. *The People's Clearance: Highland Emigration to British North America.* Winnipeg, 1982.

Campbell, Marjorie Wilkins. *McGillivray, Lord of the Northwest.* Toronto, 1962.

*Carmichael, Alexander. *Carmina Gadelica,* six volumes, Edinburgh, 1928-1971.

Chadwick, Nora K. *Celtic Britain.* London, 1963.

Clan Donald Magazines. Edinburgh.

*Clan MacLeod. *The MacLeods of Glengarry, 1793-1993.*

Collins Encyclopaedia of Scotland. Edited by John & Julia Keay. London, 1994.

Collinson, Francis. *The Traditional and National Music of Scotland.* London, 1966.

Dumbrille, Dorothy. *Up and Down the Glens: The Story of Glengarry.* Toronto, 1954.

Braggart in My Step. Toronto, 1956.

Dunbar, John Telfer. *History of Highland Dress.* Edinburgh, 1962.

Dunn, Charles. *Highland Settler.* Toronto, 1953.

Dwelly's Illustrated Gaelic to English Dictionary **(1901). Glasgow, 1994.**

Fenwick, Hubert. *The Auld Alliance.* Kineton, Warwick, 1971.

Grant, Elizabeth. *Memoirs of a Highland Lady.* Edinburgh, 1992.

Grant, Rhodes. *The Story of Martintown*, n.p. 1974.

Haldane, A.R.B. *The Drove Roads of Scotland.* Edinburgh, 1952.

*Harkness, John. *Stormont, Dundas and Glengarry,* Cornwall, 1972.

Harper, J.R. *The Fraser Highlanders.* Montreal, 1979.

*Hunter, James. *The Making of the Crofting Community.* Edinburgh, 1976. *Scottish Highlanders: A People and their Place.* **Edinburgh, 1992.** *A Dance Called America.* Edinburgh, 1994. *On the Other Side of Sorrow.* Edinburgh, 1995. *Glencoe and the Indians.* Edinburgh, 1996.

Johnson, Samuel. *A Journey to the Western Islands of Scotland.* (many editions)

MacAlpine, Neil. *A Pronouncing Gaelic-English Dictionary.* Glasgow, 1962.

MacCulloch, Donald B. *Romantic Lochaber, Arisaig and Morar.* Edinburgh, 1971.

MacCulloch, J.A. *The Misty Isle of Skye.* Stirling, 1905.

MacDonald, Donald. *Lewis: A History of the Island.* Edinburgh, 1978.

MacDonald, Norman H. *The Clan Ranald of Knoydart and Glengarry.* Edinburgh, 1979.

*Macdonell, J.A. (Greenfield). *Sketches of Glengarry in Canada.* Montreal, 1893.

*MacDonell, Margaret. *The Emigrant Experience: Songs of Highland Emigrants in North America.* Toronto, 1982.

MacKenzie, Agnes Mure. *Robert Bruce King of Scots.* Edinburgh, 1934. (And anything else by her).

*MacKay, Donald. *Scotland Farewell - The People of the Hector.* Toronto, 1980.

MacKinnon, Kenneth. *The Lion's Tongue.* Inverness, 1974.

MacLean, Calum I. *The Highlands.* 1959.

*MacLennan, Malcolm. *Gaelic Dictionary* (1925). Edinburgh, 1992.

MacLeod, Donald. *Gloomy Memories.* Toronto, 1857.

MacMillan, Sorley. *Bygone Lochaber.* Glasgow, 1971.

*MacNeil, Joe Neil. *Sgeul gu Latha, Tales until Dawn: The World of a Cape Breton Storyteller.* Translated and edited by John Shaw. Edinburgh, 1987.

MacNeil, Neil. *The Highland Heart of Nova Scotia.* Toronto, 1958.

MacPherson, Duncan. *Gateway to Skye.* Stirling, 1946.

McDonald, Rev. Fr. Allan. *Gaelic Words and Expressions from South Uist and Eriskay.* Edited by John Lorne Campbell. Dublin, 1958.

McLaren, Moray. *Lord Lovat of the '45.* London, 1957.

*McLean, Marianne. *The People of Glengarry: Highlanders in Transition, 1745-1820.* Montreal, 1991.

McLynn, Frank. *The Jacobites.* London, 1985. *Charles Edward Stuart: A Tragedy in Many Acts.* London, 1988.

McPhee, John. *The Crofter and the Laird.* New York, 1992.

Martin, M. *A. Description of the Western Islands of Scotland (1716).* Edinburgh, 1970.

Moncreiffe, Sir Iain. *The Highland Clans.* London, 1967.

Murray, W.H. *The Islands of Western Scotland.* London, 1973.

Murray, Amy. *Father Allan's Island.* Edinburgh, 1936.

Pine, L.G. *The Highland Clans: Their Origins and History.* Newton Abbot, 1972.

*Prebble, John. *Culloden,* 1967: *Glencoe,* 1968: *The Highland Clearances,* 1969: *The Lion in the North,* 1971: *Mutiny - Highland Regiments in Revolt, 1743-1804,* 1977.

Rea, F.G. *A School in South Uist.* Edited by J. L. Campbell. London, 1964.

Ross, Neil, editor, *Heroic Poetry from the book of the Dean of Lismore* (16th c.) Edinburgh, 1939.

Scott-Moncrieff, George. *The Scottish Islands.* London, 1952.

Seton, Sir Bruce & Grant, John. *The Pipes of War.* Glasgow, 1920 & 1974.

Simpson, W. Douglas. *The Historical Saint Columba.* Edinburgh, 1963.

Smout, T.C. *A History of the Scottish People.* London, 1972.

Stewart, David (of Garth). *Sketches of the Highlanders of Scotland.* Edinburgh, 1977.

Sutherland, Elizabeth. *The seer of Kintail.* London, 1974.

Thomson, Derick. *Introduction to Gaelic Poetry.* London, 1974: *The Companion to Gaelic Scotland.* 1983.

Tomasson, K. & Buist, F. *Battles of the '45.* London, 1962.

*Toomey, Kathleen. *Alexander Macdonell: The Scottish Years, 1762-1804.* Toronto 1985.

Wallace, Clarke. *Wanted: Donald Morrison - The True Story of the Megantic Outlaw.* Toronto, 1977.

Watson, J. Carmichael. *Gaelic Songs of Mary MacLeod.* Edinburgh, 1934.

Webster, David. *Scottish Highland Games.* Edinburgh, 1973.

Wood, Wendy. *Tales of the Western Isles.* Edinburgh, 1952.

Youngson, A.J. *After the Forty-Five.* Edinburgh, 1973.

About the Author

Kenneth J. McKenna has written over 300 *Highland Paths* colums for *The Glengarry News* of Alexandria, Ontario, since 1992. He has written on the music, language and traditions of the Gaelic-speaking Highland Scots for the *The Clansman* and *Celtic Heritage* of Halifax and *Am Bràighe*, the Gaelic-English publication from Cape Breton, and *The Ottawa Citizen.*
He also contributed two chapters to *The Lochaber Emigrants to Glengarry* (1994).
He lives in Glengarry County with his patient wife, Anne.